PERFORMANCE ASSESSMENT

8

Approaching Performance Assessments with Confidence

By Carol Jago

In order to get good at anything, you need to practice. Whether the goal is to improve your jump shot, level up in a video game, or make the cut in band tryouts, success requires repeated practice on the court, computer, and field. The same is true of reading and writing. The only way to get good at them is by reading and writing.

Malcolm Gladwell estimates in his book *Outliers* that mastering a skill requires about 10,000 hours of dedicated practice. He argues that individuals who are outstanding in their field have one thing in common—many, many hours of working at it. Gladwell claims that success is less dependent on innate talent than it is on practice. Now I'm pretty sure that I could put in 10,000 hours at a ballet studio and still be a terrible dancer, but I agree with Gladwell that, "Practice isn't the thing you do once you're good. It's the thing you do that makes you good."

Not just any kind of practice will help you master a skill, though. Effective practice needs to focus on improvement. That is why this series of reading and writing tasks begins with a model of the kind of reading and writing you are working towards, then takes you through practice exercises, and finally invites you to perform the skills you have practiced.

Once through the cycle is only the beginning. You will want to repeat the process many times over until close reading, supporting claims with evidence, and crafting a compelling essay is something you approach with confidence. Notice that I didn't say "with ease." I wish it were otherwise, but in my experience as a teacher and as an author, writing well is never easy.

The work is worth the effort. Like a star walking out on the stage, you put your trust in the hours you've invested in practice to result in thundering applause. To our work together!

Unit 1 Argumentative Essay
Teen Culture

STEP 1 ANALYZE THE MODEL

Should all U.S. students be required to speak at least one language besides English?

Read Source Materials

STEP 2 PRACTICE THE TASK

Should students be required to stay in school until they are 18?

Read Source Materials

Write an Argumentative Essay

STEP 3 PERFORM THE TASK

Should individuals be prosecuted for statements made on social media?

Read Source Materials

Write an Argumentative Essay

Should individuals be prosecuted for statements made on social media?

Unit 2 Informative Essay
Shaping the Earth

STEP 1 ANALYZE THE MODEL

How do nature and humans shape the earth?

Read Source Materials

© Houghton Mifflin Harcourt Publishing Company • Image Credits: ©godfer/Fotolia; ©Peter Haigh/Digital Vision/Getty Images

STEP 2 PRACTICE THE TASK

What are the effects of an earthquake?

Read Source Materials

STEP 3 PERFORM THE TASK

How do volcanoes affect people and environments?

Read Source Materials

Unit 3 Literary Analysis
Common Ground

Unit 4 Mixed Practice
On Your Own

Teen Culture

Argumentative Essay

© Houghton Mifflin Harcourt Publishing Company

STEP 1

ANALYZE THE MODEL

Evaluate an essay on whether students should learn a second language.

STEP 2

PRACTICE THE TASK

Write an essay about the requirement for students to stay in school until the age of 18.

STEP 3

PERFORM THE TASK

Write an essay on the prosecution of individuals for statements they make on social media.

Imagine you and your best friend are arguing about something. You feel that you are right, and she thinks she is correct. Did you give her reasons to prove you were right? Did she give reasons to support her thinking? Did she end up changing her opinion, or did you change yours?

You can write an argument too. You present your claim in writing, then give reasons and evidence for your point of view. What makes an argumentative essay "argumentative" is how you anticipate an opposing view, and refute it. Your goal in writing a formal argumentative essay is to convince your audience (the reader) to agree with your point of view.

IN THIS UNIT, you will learn how to write an argumentative essay that is based on your close reading and analysis of several relevant sources. You will learn a step-by-step approach to stating a claim—and then organizing your essay to support your claim in a clear and logical way.

Harnamonk

Should students be required to stay in school until they are 18?

You will read:

▶ **A LETTER**

▶ **A NEWSPAPER ARTICLE**
President Pushes States to Raise Dropout Age

▶ **A DATA ANALYSIS**
Average Income by Education, 2009

▶ **A RADIO INTERVIEW**
Paul Moran Talks with Missy Remiss on WSCH

You will write:

▶ **AN ARGUMENTATIVE ESSAY**
Should students be required to stay in school until they are 18?

Source Materials for Step 2

AS YOU READ Analyze the letter, the newspaper article, the data analysis, and the radio interview. Think about the information, including the data contained in the sources. Annotate the sources with notes that help you decide where you stand on the issue: Should students be required to stay in school until they are 18?

Source 1: Letter

November 21, 2012

Dear Grandma Ella:

I want to tell you so you don't hear from someone else—I've left school. I know this will disappoint you. I hope after you read what I have to say you will understand.

You know how hard things have been at home for the past three years with dad not working, and mom has only been able to find temporary and part-time work. I've been helping out working at Shelly's Diner, but that money does not go far.

Life was tough enough, but then the storm hit. The diner was flooded and had to close—no more job for me! Mom couldn't get to work on time since the subways were out of whack, and now she's looking for work again. The worst was my school—it took a real beating, so they relocated us to somewhere on the other side of town that takes forever to get to every day.

Rather than spend the day getting to school and back and feeling helpless, I decided to step up and look for a job to really help out at home. I was pretty lucky. I'm happy to say I found a full-time job at Marcy's, starting immediately.

Don't worry, Grandma. I know how important it is to get my education. I plan to get myself settled in this job, and then start to work on my GED. Maybe if I'm lucky and mom or dad finds a good job in the next few months I'll be able to go back to school full-time next fall. But in the meantime, I'm proud to be able to help out at home while we all try to recover from the storm.

Please understand. Thank you for everything.

Love,
Marissa

XXX

Source 2: Newspaper Article

National Education Weekly

President Pushes States to Raise Dropout Age

by Mia Lewis　　　　　　　　**January 25, 2012**

In his recent State of the Union address President Obama called on states to require students to stay in school until age 18 or graduation.

"When students don't walk away from their education, more of them walk the stage to get their diploma," the President pointed out.

This is the first time a President has weighed in on an issue that individual states are struggling to solve on their own and in their own ways. In general, the legal age for exiting school pre-graduation has been getting higher over the years. It is now age 18 in 21 states plus the District of Columbia, and age 17 in 11 other states.

Raising the age for exiting pre-graduation may not stop all dropouts, but it has a positive effect, according to New Hampshire Deputy Commissioner of Education, Paul Leather. "What it does is it sets the moral imperative so that students, parents, and educators become committed to the idea that each student will in fact graduate," Leather says.

Recently, New Hampshire raised the minimum age for exiting pre-graduation to 18. "What we found both in national and international research is that when you raise the compulsory age of education, the graduation and retention rates will in fact increase," he says.

Since the federal government covers only around 10 percent of education financing, it is unlikely to be able to force states to adopt a uniform age for exiting pre-graduation. However, for states wanting to receive special "Race to the Top" education grants, a higher pre-graduation exit age could be a requirement.

The federal government may not be able to dictate individual state policy, but it can give states a strong incentive to make sure more students graduate.

Discuss and Decide

Compare Sources 1 and 2. Explain whether or not Marissa's decision is well thought out. What is the likely effect that dropping out of school will have on her future? Cite text evidence in your discussion.

Source 3: Data Analysis

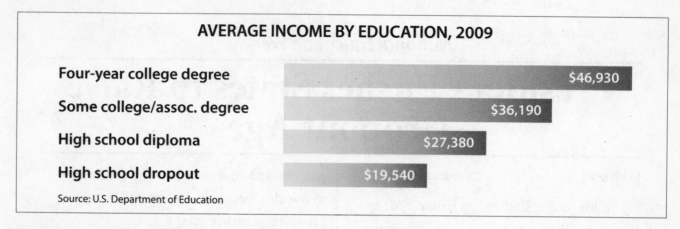

AVERAGE INCOME BY EDUCATION, 2009

Four-year college degree	$46,930
Some college/assoc. degree	$36,190
High school diploma	$27,380
High school dropout	$19,540

Source: U.S. Department of Education

Source 4: Radio Interview

Paul Moran Talks with Missy Remiss on WSCH

WSCH interviewer Paul Moran talks with Education Advocate Missy Remiss about how states are tackling high dropout rates.

WSCH: Thanks so much for being with us today. I'm going to jump right in and ask, why is everyone so worried about the high school dropout rate? What's so bad about kids deciding to leave school early?

MR: Well, the problem is that even if a student makes a reasonable decision to leave school for work, that decision is likely to have a negative impact over the course of his or her life. Those without a high school diploma have lower earnings, higher unemployment, lower job satisfaction—they even have a higher likelihood of ending up in jail or on public assistance. So, it really is a bad deal for kids.

WSCH: OK, so why not just require kids to stay in school until they are 18 or they graduate? Can't we do that? Won't that solve the problem?

MR: Well, that's really the question. 21 states plus the District of Columbia already have laws requiring students to stay in school until they are 18 or until they graduate, but some of them still have high dropout rates! And you know, forcing students to stay in school when they don't want to be there can cause problems for teachers and other students as well.

WSCH: So, raising the minimum school-leaving age doesn't automatically solve the problem?

MR: No. That's why some states have decided to take a different tack. For example, in Kentucky, they have been very successful lowering dropout rates, even though, technically, kids are allowed to leave school at age 16. They've worked hard to make schooling relevant—to offer courses that kids can see will help them get jobs and help them in their adult lives. They also have created several pathways to graduation, so there's more than one way to succeed.

WSCH: So, they're still trying to lower the dropout rate, just not by making it the law that you have to stay in school?

MR: Exactly. Everyone wants to lower the dropout rate, it's just a question of how. Now, if we could only tackle some of the economic and social problems that lead students to drop out, we'd really be able to make progress!

WSCH: Thank you so much for your time, and good luck!

Close Read

1. Cite three reasons for staying in school and getting a high school diploma.

Three reasons for staying in school and getting a highschool diploma are ~~first you~~ lower earnings, lower job satisfaction, and higher unemployment.

2. Why doesn't raising the minimum age to leave school always lead to higher graduation rates? Cite evidence in the text.

Raising the minimum age to leave school ~~always~~ doesn't raise graduation rates because ~~force~~ "forcing students to stay in school when they don't want to ~~can~~ be there can cause problems for teachers and other students."

Respond to Questions on Step 2 Sources

These questions will help you analyze the sources you've read. Use your notes and refer to the sources in order to answer the questions. Your answers to these questions will help you write your essay.

1 Evaluate the sources. Is the evidence from one source more credible than the evidence from another source? When you evaluate the credibility of a source, consider the expertise of the author and/or the organization responsible for the information. Record your reasons in the chart.

Source	Credible?	Reasons
Letter Letter to Grandma Ella	No	because it is mostly made of opinion rather than facts
Newspaper Article President Pushes States to Raise Dropout Age	Yes	because it cites it evidence
Data Analysis Average Income by Education, 2009	Yes	because it is built upon facts
Radio Interview Paul Moran Talks with Missy Remiss on WSCH	Yes	This has the evidence to prove their facts

2 Prose Constructed-Response What is the relationship between graduating high school and earning income? Cite evidence from at least two texts in your response.

3 Prose Constructed-Response Which source suggests that dropping out of school might be a valid option for some students? Cite text evidence in your response.

Types of Evidence

Every reason you offer to support the central claim of your argument must be backed up by evidence. It is useful to think ahead about evidence when you are preparing to write an argument. If there is no evidence to support your claim, you will need to revise your claim. The evidence you provide must be relevant, or directly related to your claim. It must also be sufficient. Sufficient evidence is both clear and varied.

Use this chart to help you choose different types of evidence to support your reasons.

Types of Evidence	What Does It Look Like?
Anecdotes: personal examples or stories that illustrate a point	**Letter** "Rather than spend the day getting to school and back and feeling helpless, I decided to step up and look for a job to really help out at home."
Commonly accepted beliefs: ideas that most people share	**Radio Interview** "Those without a high school diploma have lower earnings, higher unemployment, lower job satisfaction …"
Examples: specific instances or illustrations of a general idea	**Radio Interview** "… in Kentucky, they have been very successful lowering dropout rates, even though, technically, kids are allowed to leave school at age 16."
Expert opinion: statement made by an authority on the subject	**Newspaper Article** "'… sets the moral imperative so that students, parents, and educators become committed to the idea that each student will in fact graduate,' Leather says."
Facts: statements that can be proven true, such as statistics or other numerical information	**Radio interview** "21 states plus the District of Columbia already have laws requiring students to stay in school until they are 18 or until they graduate."

Write an argumentative essay to answer the question: Should students be required to stay in school until they are 18?

Planning and Prewriting

Before you draft your essay, complete some important planning steps.

Claim ⇒ Reasons ⇒ Evidence

You may prefer to do your planning on a computer.

Make a Precise Claim

1. Should students be required to stay in school until they are age 18?

yes ☐   no ☐

2. Review the evidence on pages 12–15. Do the sources support your position?

yes ☐   no ☐

3. If you answered *no* to Question 2, you can either change your position or do additional research to find supporting evidence.

4. State your claim. It should be precise. It should contain the issue and your position on the issue.

Issue: A student's age when leaving school before graduating

Your position on the issue: _____

Your precise claim: _____

State Reasons

Next, gather support for your claim. Identify several valid reasons that justify your position.

Reason 1	Reason 2	Reason 3

Find Evidence

You have identified reasons that support your claim. Summarize your reasons in the chart below. Then complete the chart by identifying evidence that supports your reasons.

Relevant Evidence: The evidence you plan to use must be *relevant* to your argument. That is, it should directly and factually support your position.

Sufficient Evidence: Additionally, your evidence must be *sufficient* to make your case. That is, you need to provide enough evidence to convince others.

Short Summary of Reasons	Evidence
Reason 1	Relevant? _____ Sufficient? _____
Reason 2	Relevant? _____ Sufficient? _____
Reason 3	Relevant? _____ Sufficient? _____

Finalize Your Plan

Whether you are writing your essay at home or working in a timed situation at school, it is important to have a plan. You will save time and create a more organized, logical essay by planning the structure before you start writing.

Use your responses on pages 18–19, as well as your close reading notes, to complete the graphic organizer.

▶ Think about how you will grab your reader's attention with an interesting fact or anecdote.

▶ Identify the issue and your position.

▶ State your precise claim.
▶ List the likely opposing claim and how you will counter it.

▶ Restate your claim.

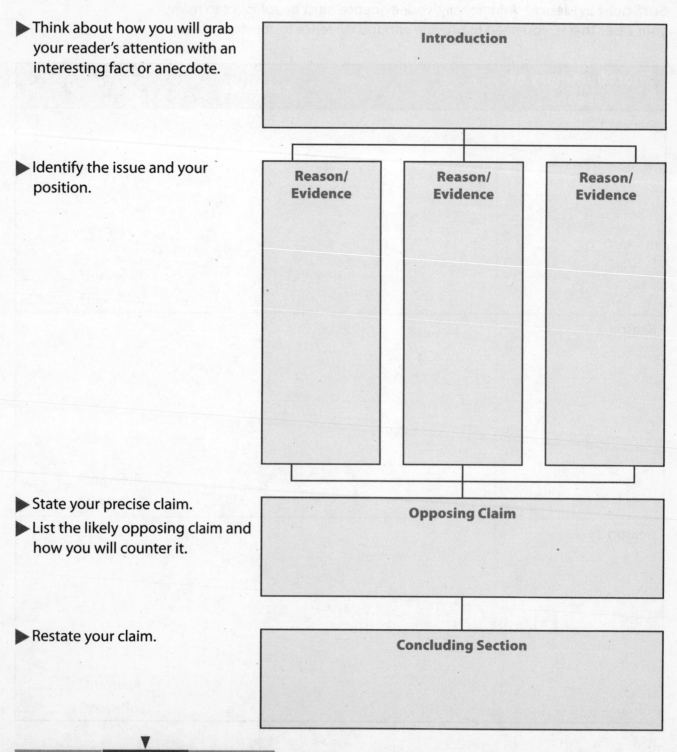

Introduction

Reason/ Evidence | **Reason/ Evidence** | **Reason/ Evidence**

Opposing Claim

Concluding Section

   1. Analyze   2. Practice   3. Perform

Draft Your Essay

As you write, think about:

▶ **Audience:** Your teacher.

▶ **Purpose:** Demonstrate your understanding of the specific requirements of an argumentative essay.

▶ **Style:** Use formal and objective tone that isn't defensive.

▶ **Transitions:** Use words such as *furthermore* or *another reason*, to create cohesion, or flow.

Revise

Revision Checklist: Self Evaluation

Use the checklist below to guide your analysis.

 If you drafted your essay on the computer, you may wish to print it out so that you can more easily evaluate it.

Ask Yourself	Tips	Revision Strategies
1. Does the introduction grab the audience's attention and include a precise claim?	Draw a wavy line under the attention-grabbing text. Bracket the claim.	Add an attention grabber. Add a claim or rework the existing one to make it more precise.
2. Do at least two valid reasons support the claim? Is each reason supported by relevant and sufficient evidence?	Underline each reason. Circle each piece of evidence, and draw an arrow to the reason it supports.	Add reasons or revise existing ones to make them more valid. Add relevant evidence to ensure that your support is sufficient.
3. Do transitions create cohesion and link related parts of the argument?	Put a star next to each transition.	Add words, phrases, or clauses to connect related ideas that lack transitions.
4. Are the reasons in the order that is most persuasive?	Number the reasons in the margin, ranking them by their strength and effectiveness.	Rearrange the reasons into a more logical order of importance.
5. Are opposing claims fairly acknowledged and refuted?	Put a plus sign by any sentence that addresses an opposing claim.	Add sentences that identify and address those opposing claims.
6. Does the concluding section restate the claim?	Put a box around the restatement of your claim.	Add a sentence that restates your claim.

Revision Checklist: Peer Review

Exchange your essay with a classmate, or read it aloud to your partner. As you read and comment on your classmate's essay, focus on logic, organization, and evidence—not on whether you agree with the author's claim. Help each other identify parts of the draft that need strengthening, reworking, or a new approach.

What To Look For	Notes for My Partner
1. Does the introduction grab the audience's attention and include a precise claim?	
2. Do at least two valid reasons support the claim? Is each reason supported by relevant and sufficient evidence?	
3. Do transitions create cohesion and link related parts of the argument?	
4. Are the reasons in the order that is most persuasive?	
5. Are opposing claims fairly acknowledged and refuted?	
6. Does the concluding section restate the claim?	

Edit

Edit your essay to correct spelling, grammar, and punctuation errors.

PERFORM THE TASK

Should individuals be prosecuted for statements made on social media?

You will read:

▶ **A RADIO INTERVIEW**
The Dangers of Cyberbullying

▶ **AN INFORMATIONAL ARTICLE**
Sacrificing the First Amendment to Catch "Cyberbullies"

▶ **A FACT SHEET**
What is Cyberbullying?

You will write:

▶ **AN ARGUMENTATIVE ESSAY**
Should individuals be prosecuted for statements made on social media?

THE DANGERS OF CYBERBULLYING

by Brett Warnke

AS YOU READ *Look for evidence that supports your position—or inspires you to change your position on this question: Should individuals be prosecuted for statements made on social media?*

NOTES

September 25, 2009 – BRETT WARNKE, moderator:

Until recently, children who were victims of bullying in the classroom or on the playground could find peace at home. But with a surge in the popularity of new technology among children and teens, bullying has become a problem that doesn't always stop at the end of the school day. As bullies turn to email, text messaging, or even social networking sites, cyberbullying has infiltrated the confines of the home, as was the case with 13-year-old Megan Meier.

10   In 2008, Lori Drew was convicted of violating the Computer Fraud and Abuse Act after creating a fake Myspace account. Assuming the fake identity of a teenage boy, Drew used the account to flirt with, and then later break up with, Megan Meier. However, the case was later appealed, and the charges lessened.

In response to the case, Congresswoman Linda Sanchez is sponsoring the Megan Meier Cyber Bullying Prevention Act. The bill would make bullying through an electronic means a federal crime. Child psychologist and strong supporter of the bill, Ms. Eden Foster, joins us today in the studio. Welcome.

20   Psychologist EDEN FOSTER: Thank you.

1. Analyze   2. Practice   3. Perform

WARNKE: Thanks for joining us. Now, what exactly does the proposed bill seek to accomplish?

FOSTER: The Megan Meier Cyber Bullying Prevention Act helps to define what is covered under the term "cyberbullying." For instance, in order for a behavior to be defined as cyberbullying, it must be repeated, hostile, and severe with the intent to embarrass, threaten, or harass. We included the term *repeated* in our definition so that actions that are a part of an isolated incident, such as telling someone you hate him or her in the
30   midst of a verbal argument, is not considered cyberbullying.

WARNKE: But shouldn't law enforcement officials be focusing on the kinds of crimes that affect more people? Cyberbullying might seem somewhat trivial, as it only affects only two people: the bully and the victim.

FOSTER: Although cyberbullying may seem insignificant in the big picture, in a survey conducted in 2006, nearly 1 in 3 teens admitted to being the victim of cyberbullying. Cyberbullying can also lead to kids getting physically injured. This bill ensures that someone is held accountable for the behavior that led to
40   someone getting hurt. And by passing the Prevention Act, we're deterring people from engaging in cyberbullying by showing such behavior is a punishable crime that won't be tolerated.

WARNKE: What are the differences between bullying and cyberbullying?

Close Read

What is a limitation of the proposed law that Ms. Foster cites?

_____

_____

_____

_____

FOSTER: Conventional bullying usually takes place between two people in the same place at the same time. On the other hand, the victim and the bully don't even need to know each other for cyberbullying to occur. It's much harder to flee a cyberbully, as they can "attack" through a variety of electronic means. The effects of cyberbullying can also reach a much wider audience, due to popularity of social networking sites.

WARNKE: But then, why don't kids just "unplug"?

FOSTER: Technology has become an essential part of our society and our homes. Use of technology has extended beyond simple entertainment. For example, teens often use their cell phones to contact their parents in emergency situations, not just to send texts with their friends or play games.

WARNKE: How has the bill been received by Congress so far?

FOSTER: There has been a lot of support in Congress from both the democratic and republican parties, not only for the Cyber Bullying Prevention Act, but also other legislation that raises community awareness about cyberbullying and ways to prevent it. I'm confident the bill will be very successful.

WARNKE: Thanks so much for coming in.

FOSTER: Thank you.

Close Read

Which is more difficult to avoid: bullying or cyberbullying? Cite text evidence to support your answer.

_____

_____

_____

_____

1. Analyze   2. Practice   3. Perform

Sacrificing the First Amendment to Catch "Cyberbullies"

October 10th, 2011 by Kirk Sigmon

For some reason, a handful of Democratic New York State senators think that the First Amendment should be treated "not as a right but as a privilege," implying that the right to free speech should essentially be revocable[1] to prevent "abuses" of free speech including "flaming" (sending angry, rude, or obscene messages to people online) and other forms of "cyberbullying." I only wish I was kidding.

NY State Senators want NY citizens to be criminally prosecuted for cyberbullying, where they define cyberbullying
10 as a plethora[2] of allegedly offensive acts on the Internet. Hilariously, the Senators include "trolling" (posting deceptive information to trick or provoke people online) and "exclusion" ("intentionally and cruelly excluding someone from an online group") as part of their definition of cyberbullying. Thus, in a sense, the Senators seem to imply that they want to not only criminally prosecute harassment and deceptive tricks posted online, but they also want to punish people for not allowing NY citizens to join their online clubs.

As you can probably imagine, I find this absolutely
20 ridiculous.

First of all, the Senators are simply mistaken about the First Amendment. Indeed, the First Amendment is regularly limited by legislation in various ways, but this does not make

---

[1] **revocable** can be recalled, withdrawn, or reversed
[2] **plethora** a superabundance, an excess

> **AS YOU READ** *Pay attention to the evidence the author presents. Jot down comments or questions about the text in the side margin.*
>
> **NOTES**

it some sort of nebulous[3] "privilege" such that hurt feelings justify its abridgement. The last time I checked, hurting someone's feelings—even in real life—never justified criminal prosecution. It usually doesn't justify civil litigation[4] without constituting outright slander[5] or libel.[6] Like it or not, implicit[7] within the text of the First Amendment is the right to be as

30 cruel as one wants, right up to the point of libel or slander.

Moreover, it is patently offensive that these Senators wish to essentially regulate the Internet. [In my opinion], regulation of the Internet to "protect" children is incredibly stupid and pointless, and a ridiculous attempt to assert US jurisdiction over the Internet generally. The idea that one could be criminally prosecuted for refusing to allow someone to join, say, a guild in a video game, is preposterous.[8] Moreover, the idea that hurt feelings justify criminal prosecution at all is an offensive use of the criminal justice system to prosecute minor

40 crimes, ultimately wasting judicial time and taxpayer resources.

The real solution to cyberbullying isn't criminal prosecution, it's education and selective participation. Children should be educated to manage and avoid offensive situations on the Internet. If the child in question can't handle that, they should not use the Internet. It's that simple.

---

[3] **nebulous** lacking definite form or limits, vague
[4] **litigation** a contested or argued legal proceeding
[5] **slander** oral communication of false statements that damages a person's reputation
[6] **libel** a false publication that damages a person's reputation
[7] **implicit** implied or understood though not directly expressed
[8] **preposterous** contrary to nature, reason, or common sense, absurd, foolish

Close Read

The senators define *exclusion* as "intentionally and cruelly excluding someone from an online group." Why might the author find this "absolutely ridiculous"? Cite text evidence in your response.

Source 3: Fact Sheet

What is Cyberbullying?

Willful and repeated harm inflicted through the use of computers, cell phones, and other electronic devices[1]

Cyberbullying includes:

- Writing hurtful statements on a social media site or website
- Forwarding rumors and gossip through text messages or emails
- Posting embarrassing pictures of someone online
- Digitally editing and distributing pictures of another person
- Flaming, insulting, or slandering others in a public area online
- Pretending to be another person online
- Setting up fake user accounts to stalk, harass, or embarrass others
- Anytime technology is used to harm another person!

The Ophelia Project identifies two main contributors to the hurtful impact of cyberbullying:

1. **Empathetic Disconnect:**
   This describes the inability to sense the emotions and feelings associated with the receipt of a message. In traditional bullying, an aggressor immediately sees the hurt they have caused the target. The lack of immediate emotional feedback in cyberbullying allows an aggressor to often continue the hurtful behaviors unchecked. Also, due to the ability to maintain anonymity on the Internet, an aggressor and target may never know each other or interact face-to-face.

2. **The Infinite Bystander Effect:**
   In a traditional bullying situation, the number of bystanders is limited to whoever is present at the time of the incident. With cyberbullying, the aggression remains present online and can be viewed by anyone with access to the web.

Cyberbullying Fast Facts

According to Cyberbullying Research Center[1]:

- Estimates on the prevalence of cyberbullying vary from **10-40%** or more.
- **20%** of youth ages 11-18 have been a victim of cyberbullying
- **10%** of youth ages 11-18 have been both a victim and offender

60% of targets said that their online experiences as a target of cyberbullying affected them at school, home, and with friends, and reported experiencing feelings of frustration, anger and sadness[2]

84% of cyberbullies report to know their target[3]

When teens were asked why they think others cyberbully, **81%** said that cyberbullies think it is funny.[4]

45% of young people (ages 14-24) reported that they see people being mean to each other on social networking sites.[5]

References:
[1]Cyberbullying Research Center. www.cyberbullying.us (accessed: February, 2011)
[2]Patchin, J. W. & Hinduja, S. (2006). Bullies move beyond the schoolyard: A preliminary look at cyberbullying. *Youth Violence and Juvenile Justice, 4*(2), 123-147.
[3]Ybarra, M.L., & Mitchell, K.J. (2004). Online aggressor/targets, aggressors, and targets: A comparison of associated youth characteristics. *Journal of Child Psychology and Psychiatry, 45*(7), 1308-1316
[4]National Crime Prevention Council http://www.ncpc.org/cyberbullying (accessed: March, 2011)
[5]A Thin Line: 2009 AP-MTV Digital Abuse Study. http://www.athinline.org/MTV-AP_Digital_Abuse_Study_Executive_Summary.pdf

Discuss and Decide

Which fact in the sheet most strongly indicates that cyberbullying is a serious problem? Cite text evidence in your discussion.

Respond to Questions on Step 3 Sources

These questions will help you think about the sources you've read and viewed. Use your notes and refer to the sources in order to answer the questions. Your answers to these questions will help you write your essay.

1 Is the evidence from one source more credible than the evidence from another source? When you evaluate the credibility of a source, consider the expertise of the author and/or the organization responsible for the information. Record your reasons.

Source	Credible?	Reasons
Radio Interview The Dangers of Cyberbullying		
Informational Article Sacrificing the First Amendment to catch "Cyberbullies"		
Fact Sheet What is Cyberbullying?		

2 **Prose Constructed-Response** You have read three texts about cyberbullying. All three take a position on cyberbullying. Analyze the strengths of the arguments made in at least two of the texts. Remember to use textual evidence to support your ideas.

_____

_____

_____

_____

_____

_____

Part 2: Write

Plan

Use the graphic organizer to help you outline the structure of your argumentative essay.

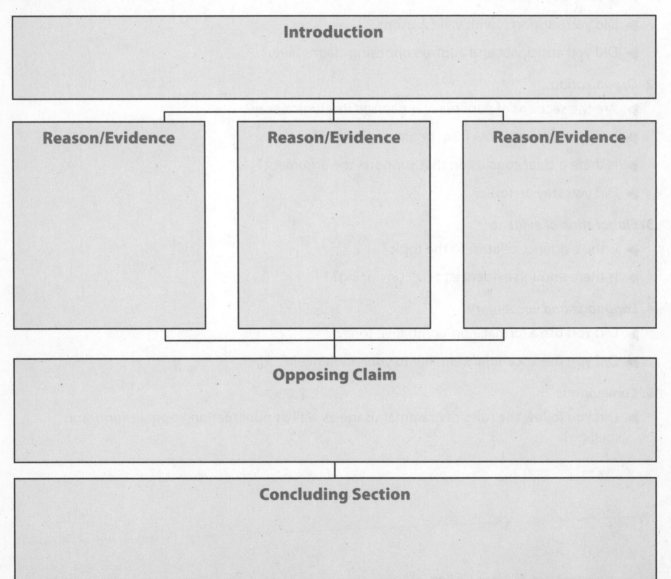

Introduction

Reason/Evidence	Reason/Evidence	Reason/Evidence

Opposing Claim

Concluding Section

Draft

 Use your notes and completed graphic organizer to write a first draft of your argumentative essay.

Revise and Edit

 Look back over your essay and compare it to the Evaluation Criteria. Revise your essay and edit it to correct spelling, grammar, and punctuation errors.

Evaluation Criteria

Your teacher will be looking for:

1. *Statement of purpose*

▶ Is your claim specific?

▶ Did you support it with valid reasons?

▶ Did you anticipate and address opposing claims fairly?

2. *Organization*

▶ Are the sections of your essay organized in a logical way?

▶ Is there a smooth flow from beginning to end?

▶ Is there a clear conclusion that supports the argument?

▶ Did you stay on topic?

3. *Elaboration of evidence*

▶ Is the evidence relative to the topic?

▶ Is there enough evidence to be convincing?

4. *Language and vocabulary*

▶ Did you use a formal, non-combative tone?

▶ Did you use vocabulary familiar to your audience?

5. *Conventions*

▶ Did you follow the rules of grammar usage as well as punctuation, capitalization, and spelling?

Shaping the Earth

Informative Essay

An informative or expository essay is meant to communicate factual information about a topic. An informative essay is classified as nonfiction. Newspapers and magazines are two places that often feature nonfiction work. With today's technology, you have access to nonfiction writing at the click of a mouse, to read information on the Internet.

The nonfiction topics that you will read about in this unit describe real events that occur in nature. These events help shape the way the earth looks.

IN THIS UNIT, you will analyze information from nonfiction articles, blogs, a news report, and an insurance claim. You will study a variety of text structures that are frequently used in the writing of informative texts. You will use these text structures to plan and write your essays.

STEP 1

ANALYZE THE MODEL

Analyze two informative essays about the impact of humans on the planet.

STEP 2

PRACTICE THE TASK

Write an informative essay about the effects of earthquakes.

STEP 3

PERFORM THE TASK

Write an informative essay on the effects of volcanoes.

How do nature and humans shape the earth?

You will read:

▶ **AN INSTRUCTIONAL ARTICLE**
Get Organized

You will analyze:

▶ **TWO STUDENT MODELS**
Erosion by Nature

How Humans Shape the Earth

Source Materials for Step 1

Ms. Chen's students read the following text to help them learn strategies for writing informative essays. As you read, underline information that you find useful.

Get Organized

by Matthew Reilly

An informative essay lets you expand and share your knowledge of a topic. This type of writing assignment requires you to research, plan, and write a clearly organized essay that presents a central idea, supported by details, facts, and explanations.

A structure is a system in which the parts all have a function. When you write an essay, the parts should *relate* to each other in a clear way to support your message. Graphic organizers can help you plan your organizational structure.

Main Idea and Supporting Details

The success of your informative essay will depend on your main idea and supporting details. In the graphic organizer below, jot down your main idea or central point. Then identify the details you will use to support or explain your main idea.

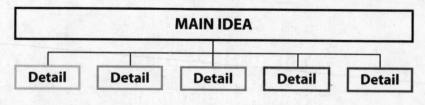

Cause-and Effect-Organization

Cause-and-effect writing explains why something happened, why something exists, or what resulted from an action or condition. The way cause-and-effect writing is organized depends on your topic and purpose for writing. Different types of cause-and-effect organization are shown below.

1. Cause-to-Effect Organization

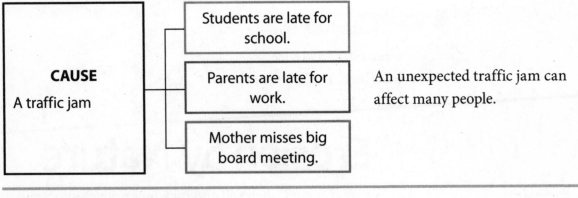

CAUSE A traffic jam	Students are late for school.	An unexpected traffic jam can affect many people.
	Parents are late for work.	
	Mother misses big board meeting.	

2. Effect-to-Cause Organization

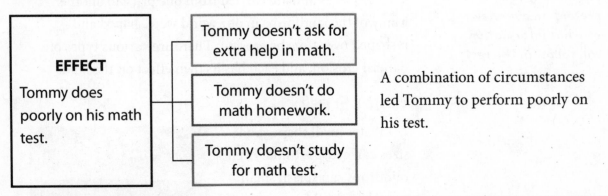

EFFECT Tommy does poorly on his math test.	Tommy doesn't ask for extra help in math.	A combination of circumstances led Tommy to perform poorly on his test.
	Tommy doesn't do math homework.	
	Tommy doesn't study for math test.	

3. Causal Chain

In a causal chain, one event causes the next event to occur. The second event causes the third event, which causes the fourth. You may use a causal chain to explain why a series of events took place.

Discuss and Decide

Which text structure would be more helpful in discussing how a car works?

Analyze Two Student Models for Step 1

Cassandra used a cause-and-effect text structure for her essay. Read her essay closely. The red side notes are comments made by her teacher, Ms. Chen.

Cassandra's Model

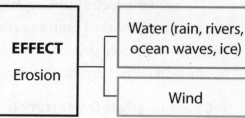

EFFECT Erosion	Water (rain, rivers, ocean waves, ice)
	Wind

Cassandra Lawrence
Ms. Chen, English
March 12

Erosion by Nature

Erosion occurs when soil and rock break down into smaller pieces and are carried from one place to another. Many of the landforms in our world were shaped and reshaped over time by erosion. There are various types of natural erosion, and each has its own effect on the land.

Good opening paragraph. You present an overview of what information will follow in the rest of your essay.

Water Erosion

Water in all shapes and sizes can cause erosion. Even raindrops can splash small particles of soil from one place to another. When it rains, water flows down hill, sometimes making gullies. Each time it rains, the gullies get bigger. The water flowing into the gullies carries soil particles. The soil gets into rivers and is carried far away.

Canyons are formed by the erosion caused by a river.

As rivers flow over time, they can gradually wear down not only soil but rock as well, as evidenced by the ravines and cliffs that some rivers flow through. The constant flow of the water shapes the rock and shapes the earth. Ocean waves crashing into the shore are also a powerful force. They shape the beaches, rocks, cliffs, and coastline, year after year.

Ice is another form of water that shapes the earth through erosion. Huge glaciers crush and scrape rock as they slowly move. Bits of rock are also taken up into the glacier as the water at the bottom freezes and melts and freezes again. Even if it's not in a glacier, when water in a crack of stone freezes, the crack gets bigger and then eventually the rock will break apart.

Nice example! Ice does not always come to mind when we think of erosion.

Wind Erosion

Wind erosion is a powerful force, especially in dry desert areas. The wind picks up grains of sand and blows them around. In some places, the wind piles up sand in one area creating a huge dune, and then shifts the dunes from place to place. The sand and other particles in the air also bang into the land, wearing away rocks and hills, changing their shape bit by bit. Some rocks in the desert have transformed into amazing and strange shapes (mushrooms, arches) as they have been sculpted by the wind and sand over hundreds and thousands of years

Your paragraphs all clearly show how each natural element causes erosion.

Erosion happens slowly, but over time it can bring about enormous changes in the shape of the land.

Discuss and Decide

What type of cause-effect organization is used in this essay? Why is this an effective way to present information on erosion?

Trevor chose to use a main idea/detail text structure for his essay. Ms. Chen made her notes in red.

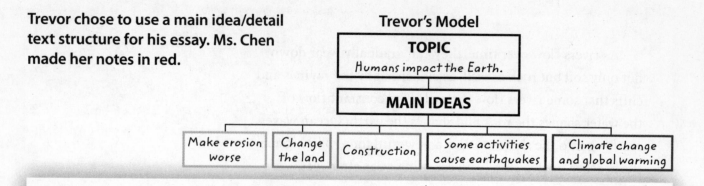

Trevor's Model

TOPIC
Humans impact the Earth.

MAIN IDEAS

| Make erosion worse | Change the land | Construction | Some activities cause earthquakes | Climate change and global warming |

Trevor Kelley
Ms. Chen, English
March 12

How Humans Shape the Earth

Strong introduction. It catches my interest.

It's not just natural forces such as volcanoes, earthquakes, wind, water, and ice that shape the earth. Humans also have an impact on the Earth, and it is not always a good one.

One way humans shape the earth is by making erosion worse. Many human activities cause erosion. Some, such as large-scale agriculture, can change weeds, grasses, shrubs, and trees whose roots hold the soil in place. Removing all these and then plowing up the land to plant crops means it is easier for rain to wash soil particles away. The topsoil that is washed away clogs rivers and streams and causes other problems downstream. Loss of topsoil also means the fields are not as fertile and won't grow as many crops.

These details support the topic sentence nicely.

Human activity affects the Earth by changing the land. For example, deforestation, or clearing land of trees, is harmful because trees provide many benefits. Trees stop erosion, keep temperatures down, and conserve the soil's water and nutrients. Another problem that humans cause is desertification, which occurs when land loses its plants and wildlife and becomes desert. Deserts don't support much life and can't easily be used to grow food.

1. Analyze   2. Practice   3. Perform

Construction has a huge impact on the Earth. Think of all the buildings, roads, parking lots, bridges, and dams that people have built over the centuries. The cement and tarmac surfaces of roofs and roads retain heat and channel or absorb water in a different way from soil and plants, but do not release them back into the environment. Soil and plants use heat and water to grow more plants. In this way, human-built structures affect the Earth differently than natural elements.

People are very clever and can do amazing things, but they can't always predict the results of their actions. For example, there is evidence that some mining and drilling activities (such as fracking) can cause small earthquakes. The shifts in the Earth that result from earthquakes further change the landscape. Burning fossil fuels (coal, petroleum, natural gas) and cutting down trees remove valuable resources that cannot be replaced and change the way these areas appear.

Probably the biggest (unpredicted) impact that humans are having on the earth is climate change and global warming. This is happening at least partly because of human activity such as burning fossil fuels and deforestation. Climate change means that all kinds of weather patterns are becoming less predictable and more extreme. The good news is that if people are smart enough to create climate change, they should be smart enough to figure out a solution.

Your paragraphs have clear topic sentences. This organization makes it easy for the reader to follow along.

Good way to connect your final summary to your opening paragraph.

Discuss and Decide

Could a cause-and-effect organization be used with this topic? If so, which model would work best?

Terminology of Informative Texts

Read each term and explanation. Then look back at and analyze each student model. Find an example to complete the chart. Make a claim about which model was more successful in illustrating each term.

Term	Explanation	Example from Student Models
topic	The **topic** is a word or phrase that tells what the essay is about.	
text structure	The **text structure** is the organizational pattern of an essay.	
main idea	The **main idea** is the controlling, or overarching, idea that states the main point the writer chooses to make.	
supporting evidence	The **supporting evidence** is relevant quotations and concrete details that support the main idea.	
domain-specific vocabulary	**Domain-specific vocabulary** is content-specific words that are not generally used in conversation.	
text features	**Text features** are features that help organize the text, such as: headings, boldface type, italic type, bulleted or numbered lists, sidebars, and graphic aids, including charts, tables, timelines, illustrations, and photographs.	

Claim:_____

Support your claim by citing text evidence.

_____

_____

What are the effects of an earthquake?

You will read:

▶ **AN INFORMATIVE BROCHURE**
If You Travelled to Gondwana...

▶ **A BLOG**
A Rough Commute

▶ **A NEWS REPORT**
Loma Prieta Earthquake

▶ **AN INSURANCE CLAIM**

You will write:

▶ **A CAUSE-AND-EFFECT ESSAY**
What are the effects of an earthquake?

Source Materials for Step 2

AS YOU READ You will be writing an informative essay about earthquakes. Carefully study the sources in Step 2. Annotate by underlining and circling information that may be useful to you when you write your essay.

Source 1: Informative Brochure

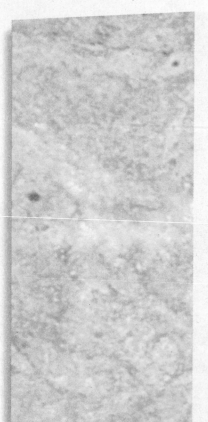

If you Traveled to Gondwana . . .

Do you wish you could ride your bike to Europe? Would you like to grow palm trees in Antarctica? Well, a mere 200 million years ago, you could have.

Ancient History

Earth's continents are not fixed in place. Rather, they slide slowly over the planet's molten mantle, colliding and separating, creating new landforms. The process is not gentle. Where two continental plates meet, mountains form, earthquakes rattle, and volcanoes erupt. Where continental plates slide apart, the consequences are no less drastic. Oceans pour in, and plants and animals that once lived together become isolated.

The lands of the southern hemisphere—South America, Africa, Australia, India, and Antarctica—were once united in the supercontinent Gondwana.

When continental plates move away from each other, huge rifts occur and ocean water spills in. These shifting seas take ocean life with it, so it's possible to find certain species—such as fish—who have been isolated from their original habitat.

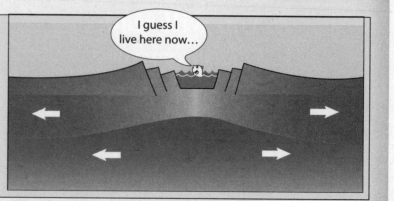

I guess I live here now...

Ancient Ancestors

- The llama of South America is related to the camel of Africa. How could this be? How could either species cross the Atlantic Ocean? They didn't. The ancestor of llamas and camels lived on Gondwana—before the supercontinent split apart.

- Fossil discoveries show that the platypus has only lived in two far-flung places: in Australia and in Argentina, countries which were joined before the supercontinent broke apart.

- Even blind, cave-dwelling goby fish were scattered by Gondwana's split. Scientists recently learned that a species of goby native to Madagascar is related to a species of goby in Australia—6,000 kilometers away!

Who knows where the continents will end up 200 million years from now. Maybe some long-lost relatives, such as goby fish, can reunite!

Two contemporary species of goby fish—one native to Madagascar and the other to Australia—are said to have separated from from a goby species living in Gondwana.

250 million years ago, the Tethys Sea flowed in to divide the super-continent Pangaea into Laurasia in the north and Gondwana in the south.

100 million years ago

Today

Close Read

Explain what causes movement in the Earth's continents. Cite textual evidence in your response.

Source 2: Blog

EYEWITNESS REPORT

A Rough Commute

Steven Nguyen
Sacramento, California

3:38 pm

Traffic on Franklin Boulevard is barely crawling, and every lane is packed. It's like an early rush hour, only going in both directions.

3:55 pm

We all stop as a convoy of screaming fire engines and ambulances makes its way north. I try to call home again. No luck—just a beep-beep-beep busy signal. Everybody in California must be trying to call home now, and the telecommunications system is overwhelmed. The car radio isn't much help. Most of the dial is static; only a few stations are still transmitting. Somebody says the quake measured 7.8 on the Richter scale, with an epicenter 15 miles east.

4:29 pm

Northbound traffic on Franklin Boulevard comes to a grinding halt. I give up and turn west onto Stockton Street.

5:05 pm

A huge cloud of blue smoke is rising to the east. Sirens wail in all directions. Helicopters clatter across the sky.

5:18 pm

The traffic on Stockton stops moving, so I take some side streets and try the freeway. I should have been suspicious by the lack of cars. Within seconds, I have to slam on the brakes. A section of asphalt six lanes wide has been tilted up like a castle drawbridge. I get out of the car and gasp. The scar of the quake is plain to see—a jagged line of raw earth tracing across miles of tomato fields. No way forward. I climb back in my car and turn around.

Welcome!
About/FAQ
Surprise me!
Subscribe by Email

SEARCH

Archives

2013
2012
2011
2010

Discuss and Decide

What details in this blog help you picture the events described here? Cite textual evidence in your response.

1. Analyze   2. Practice   3. Perform

LOMA PRIETA EARTHQUAKE

San Francisco, CA   **October 18, 1989**

by Olivia Esposito

The earthquake struck at 5:04 P.M., while the San Francisco Giants and Oakland Athletics were warming up for the third game of the 1989 World Series. With an epicenter near Santa Cruz, about 50 miles to the south, the quake measured 7.1 on the Richter Scale and shook the ground for 15 seconds. Although the players and fans at Candlestick Park were understandably frightened, the stadium stood and nobody was injured.

Across the region, others were not so lucky. The earthquake killed more than 60 people, injured almost 4,000, and left several thousand Californians homeless. A span of the Bay Bridge collapsed, tens of thousands of buildings were damaged or destroyed, and the final repair bill came to $6 billion.

Much of the destruction centered on the region's roadways, and some of the worst damage occurred to a raised section of Interstate 880 in Oakland. This double-deck freeway had been built in

The Loma Prieta earthquake took place during the World Series in 1989.

the 1950s and reinforced for earthquakes in the 1970s. Unfortunately this part of the structure was built on reclaimed marshland. During the earthquake, the soil liquefied. The freeway buckled, support columns failed, and the upper deck crashed onto the first deck, killing 41 people in their cars.

Some observers think that the World Series saved lives that day. Many office workers went home early to watch the game on TV, while countless others walked to restaurants to see the game. As a result, fewer cars were on the road, and an untold number of drivers avoided catastrophe.

Discuss and Decide

What was the most destructive effect of the Loma Prieta earthquake? Cite textual evidence in your response.

Source 4: Insurance Claim

Earthquake Insurance Claim Form		
Policy Holder Sandra T. Upton		**Insurance Company** Alphabets, LLC
Address 5231 Live Oak Way, Los Gatos, CA		**Policy Identification Number** 0221-95550123
Covered Property (same)		**Earthquake Date** 10/17/89
Item	**Damage**	**Estimated Repair/ Replacement Cost**
driveway	concrete buckled and cracked	$3,200
chimney/fireplace	partially collapsed	$5,000
front porch	support columns askew	$2,800
hallway	east wall cracked in three places	$4,100
kitchen	window broken, counters cracked, ceiling collapsed	$7,250
bedroom	window broken, closet walls cracked, floor displaced	$9,300
bathroom	shower wall cracked, sink crushed, toilet broken, ceiling collapsed	$8,600
front room	windows broken, window frames dislodged, ceiling cracked	$5,490
garage	windows broken, wall cracked	$1,900
appliances	hot-water heater, refrigerator, stove, oven, television destroyed	$5,740
backyard	porch buckled, approximately half of fence collapsed	$1,500
	Total	$54,880

Discuss and Decide

Which details from the insurance claim help you better understand the scope and cost of an earthquake's destructiveness? Cite evidence from the claim form in your response.

Respond to Questions on Step 2 Sources

The following questions will help you think about the sources you've read. Use your notes and refer to the sources as you answer the questions. Your answers to will help you write your essay.

1 Who was the least impacted by the Loma Prieta Earthquake?

    a. people on the Bay Bridge

    b. people in the Oakland area

    c. people in Candlestick Park

    d. people near the freeway

2 Which words best support your answer to Question 1?

    a. "Many office workers went home early to watch the game on TV, while countless others walked to bars and restaurants to see the game."

    b. "The freeway buckled, support columns failed, and the upper deck crashed onto the first deck, killing 41 people in their cars."

    c. "Although the players and fans at Candlestick Park were understandably frightened, the stadium stood and nobody was injured."

    d. "A span of the Bay Bridge collapsed, tens of thousands of buildings were damaged or destroyed, and the final repair bill came to $7 billion."

3 Which of these is an effect of continental plates meeting?

   a. oceans pour in

   b. mountains form

   c. plants and animals become isolated

   d. people move to different continents

4 Which damages were the most costly in Sandra T. Upton's home?

   a. broken windows/cracked wall in the garage and support columns on the front porch

   b. buckled porch/collapsed fence in backyard and east wall cracked in hallway

   c. broken window/collapsed ceiling in kitchen and cracked shower wall/broken toilet in bathroom

   d. replacement of appliances and cracked closet walls/displaced floor in bedroom

5 What information about earthquakes can you learn from the insurance claim mentioned in Question 4 that you could you not get from the other sources?

   a. The Richter Scale is the standard by which earthquake severity is measured.

   b. Earthquakes can cause a lot of damage to people even if they are not injured.

   c. Earthquakes can split the ground open.

   d. Earth's continents aren't fixed in place.

6 **Prose Constructed-Response** What is the main idea of "If You Travelled to Gondwana…"? What details best support it? Cite evidence from the text in your response.

_____

_____

_____

_____

_____

_____

_____

_____

_____

7 **Prose Constructed-Response** Which selection is most effective in showing the effects of earthquakes? Why? Cite evidence from the texts in your response.

_____

_____

_____

_____

_____

_____

_____

_____

_____

Write a cause-and-effect essay that answers the question:
What are the effects of an earthquake?

Planning and Prewriting

When you write a cause-and-effect essay, you can usually choose from a cause-to-effect organization, an effect-to-cause organization, or a causal chain. For your essay on earthquakes, you will use a cause-to-effect organization.

 You may prefer to do your planning on the computer.

Decide on Cause and Effects

Based on details and evidence presented in the sources, what are the effects of earthquakes? List them below.

Cause: Earthquakes

Effects:

_____

_____

_____

_____

Organize the Effects

Effects on the Earth:

_____

Effects on people:

_____

Effects on property:

_____

Find Evidence

For each type of effect, cite evidence that it was caused by an earthquake.

Effect	Evidence

Finalize Your Plan

Use your responses and notes from previous pages to create a detailed plan for your essay.

- ▶ Hook your audience with an interesting detail, question, or quotation.
- ▶ Provide any background information needed.
- ▶ Follow a framework like the one shown here to organize your main ideas and supporting evidence.

- ▶ State each effect concisely.
- ▶ Include relevant facts, concrete details, and other evidence for each effect.
- ▶ Make the nature of the cause-and-effect relationship clear.

- ▶ Summarize the key cause and effects.
- ▶ Include an observation about why the information is important.

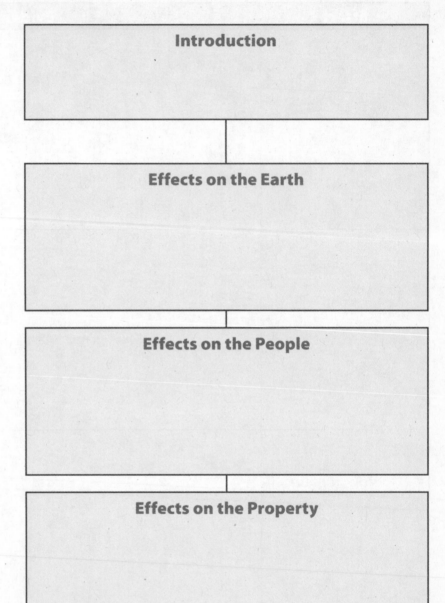

Introduction

Effects on the Earth

Effects on the People

Effects on the Property

Conclusion

Draft Your Essay

As you write, think about:

▶ **Audience:** Your teacher

▶ **Purpose:** Demonstrate your understanding of the specific requirements of an informative essay.

▶ **Style:** Use a formal and objective tone.

▶ **Transitions:** Use words and phrases such as *because* or *so* to create cohesion, or flow.

Revise

Revision Checklist: Self Evaluation

Use the checklist below to guide your analysis.

 If you drafted your essay on the computer, you may wish to print it out so that you can more easily evaluate it.

Ask Yourself	Tips	Revision Strategies
1. Does the introduction grab the audience's attention?	Underline sentences in the introduction that engage readers.	Add an interesting question, fact, or observation to get the reader's attention.
2. Is each cause and its effect supported by textual evidence, facts, and concrete details?	Circle textual evidence.	Add textual evidence if necessary.
3. Are appropriate and varied transitions used to make the cause and its effects clear?	Place a checkmark next to each transitional word or phrase.	Add transitional words or phrases where needed to clarify the relationships between ideas.
4. Does the concluding section sum up ideas? Does it give the audience something to think about?	Double underline the summary of key points in the concluding section. Underline the insight offered to readers.	Add an overarching view of key points or a final observation about the significance of the cause and its effects.

Revision Checklist: Peer Review

Exchange your essay with a classmate, or read it aloud to your partner. As you read and comment on your classmate's essay, focus on how clearly the causes of earthquakes and their effects have been presented. Help each other identify parts of the drafts that need strengthening, reworking, or even a complete new approach.

What To Look For	Notes for My Partner
1. Does the introduction grab the audience's attention?	
2. Is each cause and its effect supported by textual evidence, facts, and concrete details?	
3. Are appropriate and varied transitions used to make the cause and its clear?	
4. Does the concluding section sum up ideas? Does it give the audience something to think about?	

Edit

Edit your essay to correct spelling, grammar, and punctuation errors.

How do volcanoes affect people and environments?

You will read:

▶ **THREE INFORMATIONAL ARTICLES**

How Many Active Volcanoes Are There?

Volcanic Soils

On the Slopes of Mauna Loa, Hawaii Island

You will write:

▶ **AN INFORMATIVE ESSAY**
How do volcanoes affect people and environments?

How Many Active Volcanoes Are There?

by Tom Simkin and Lee Siebert, Smithsonian Institution, Global Volcanism Program

NOTES

The answer to this common question depends upon the use of the word "active." At least 20 volcanoes will probably be erupting as you read these words (Italy's Stromboli, for example, has been erupting for more than a thousand years). Roughly 60 erupted each year through the 1990s; 154 in the full decade of 1990–1999; about 550 have had historically documented eruptions. Some 1300 (and perhaps more than 1500) have erupted in the Holocene (the past 10,000 years), and some estimates of young seafloor volcanoes exceed a

10 million. Because dormant intervals between major eruptions at a single volcano may last hundreds to thousands of years, dwarfing the relatively short historical record in many regions, it is misleading to restrict usage of "active volcano" to recorded human memories: we prefer to add another identifying word (e.g.[1] "historically active" or "Holocene volcano").

The definition of "volcano" is as important in answering the number question as the definition of "active." Usage has varied widely, with "volcano" applied to individual vents, measured in meters, through volcanic edifices[1] measured in

20 tens of kilometers, to volcanic fields measured in hundreds of kilometers. We have tended toward the broader definition

---

[1] **edifice:** cone-shaped structure at a volcano's top
[2] **e.g.:** *exempli gratia,* Latin for "for example"

in our compilations, allowing the record of a single large plumbing system[3] to be viewed as a whole, but this approach often requires careful work in field and laboratory to establish the integrity of a group's common magmatic[4] link. The problem is particularly difficult in Iceland, where eruptions separated by many tens of kilometers along a single rift may share the same magmatic system. A "volcanic field," such as Mexico's Michoacán-Guanajuato field (comprising nearly 1,400 cinder
30 cones[5], maars[6], and shield volcanoes[7] derived from a single magmatic system, dotting a 200 x 250 km area) may be counted the same as a single volcanic edifice. Perhaps the most honest answer to the number question is that we do not really have an accurate count of the world's volcanoes, but that there are at least a thousand identified magma systems[8]—on land alone— likely to erupt in the future.

How many active volcanoes known?

Erupting now:	perhaps 20
Each year:	50-70
Each decade:	about 160
Historical eruptions:	about 550
Known Holocene eruptions (last 10,000 years):	about 1300
Known (and possible) Holocene eruptions:	about 1500

Note that these figures do *not* include the large number of eruptions (and undescribed volcanoes) on the deep sea floor.

---

[3] **single large plumbing system:** underground chambers of liquid magma that run beneath volcanoes in a series of "pipes"

[4] **magmatic:** made of molten rock found under the earth's crust

[5] **cinder cone:** the simplest type of volcano, created when particles and blobs of congealed lava explode from one vent. Cinder cones have a circular or oval cone around their vent.

[6] **maar:** depressed crater caused by an eruption during which ground water makes contact with lava or magma, resulting in an explosion. The explosion makes a hole in the ground, which is the maar crater.

[7] **shield volcano:** large volcanoes that are built almost completely from lava. They are named for their sloping sides, which resemble a warrior's shield.

[8] **magma system:** the underground sysstem of "pipes" through which magma flows

Close Read

What is the best answer to the title's question? Cite textual evidence in your response.

Source 2: Informational Article

Volcanic Soils

by Russell McDonaugh

AS YOU READ *Take notes about the use of volcanic soils.*

NOTES

Volcanic eruptions produce deposits of rock and ash in the surrounding area. These deposits are rich in minerals, but the minerals are not immediately available to plants. Depending on the location of the volcano, it can take thousands of years of weathering for the ash and rock deposits to form a rich soil. When they do become soils, they are often among the richest soils on Earth.

The rate at which volcanic loam is formed often depends on geographical factors. In Hawaii, for example, weathering from
10 wind and rain occurs quickly because of the tropical climate. Hawaii's lush vegetation is due to the rapid formation of soil from volcanic deposits. Ash also contributes to soil formation. However, smaller particles of ash—often less than a millimeter in diameter—are more quickly embedded in the existing soil and more quickly broken down into nutrients. These smaller particles of ash are usually found farther from the volcano than larger particles.

Once volcanic deposits have been broken down, they enrich the soil both by adding important nutrients for plants and
20 by providing excellent drainage. The extent to which these deposits enrich the soil is well-illustrated in Italy. The soil in southern Italy is generally quite poor except for the area around Naples. This region includes Mount Vesuvius, which experienced two major eruptions more than 10,000 years ago.

This area has been intensively cultivated for crops for over 2,000 years. The soil is so rich that farmers often plant different crops intermingled with each other to maximize the use of every square inch available.

In addition to enriching soil nutrients, volcanic deposits
30 improve soil in other ways. By improving moisture retention, they make soil easier to till for farming. Also, volcanic soils are good for pasture growth because of how well they hold water for plants. The North Island of New Zealand, which is rich in volcanic loam, has a large and prosperous dairy industry that depends on the verdant pasturelands of the island.

A stamp printed in 1996 shows Pukekura Park Gardens in New Plymouth, a major regional city on the North Island of New Zealand. New Plymouth is known for having rich volcanic soil and lush gardens. The stamp shows a still-active volcano in the background, Mt. Taranaki.

Close Read

Why is it important to know that the soil in southern Italy is unusually poor? Cite text evidence in your response.

_____

_____

_____

On the Slopes of
Mauna Loa, Hawaii Island

AS YOU READ *Underline key ideas and evidence that you might use in your essay.*

NOTES

Highway 11 is the route a traveler would normally follow from the Kona (west side) direction and driving towards the Hawaii Volcanoes National Park. The western slopes from Manuka State Park to the entrance to the Kahuku section of the Hawaii Volcanoes National Park feature a forest reserve and broad vistas with sweeping views of the ocean and mountain. This section includes landscape passing over relatively new lava so the traveler can experience transitions from substantially untouched to well vegetated volcanic terrain and rain forest.

10 The southern slopes from Kahuku to the county park at Honuapo Bay include the green segment that winds into the Waiohinu Valley then down towards the ocean, with a panorama that may extend to a distant view of the Kilauea volcano. The eastern slopes cover the area from Honuapo to the main entrance to the Hawaii Volcanoes National park and offer long, sweeping green views towards the Mauna Loa summit as well as the spectacular and unusual Ninole Hills. The road rises from sea level to over 4,000 feet and is partly within the boundary of the Hawaii Volcanoes National Park. The Kau
20 Scenic Byway offers by far the longest stretches of unspoiled natural scenery to be found anywhere in the inhabited Hawaiian Islands.

Discuss and Decide

What is the effect of volcanoes on Mauna Loa? Cite textual evidence in your response.

▼

1. Analyze   2. Practice   3. Perform

Respond to Questions on Step 3 Sources

The following questions will help you think about the sources you've read. Use your notes and refer to the sources as you answer the questions. Your answers to will help you write your essay.

1 Why is volcanic soil important to those in the region around Naples?

 a. It is the only place scientists can study volcanic ash.

 b. It makes rich soil that is used to grow many plants.

 c. It provides pastureland that supports a dairy industry.

 d. It makes the area unappealing to tourists.

2 Which words best support your answer to Question 1?

 a. "... weathering from wind and rain occurs quickly because of the tropical climate."

 b. "... prosperous dairy industry that depends on the verdant pasturelands ..."

 c. "... farmers often plant different crops ..."

 d. "... minerals are not immediately available to plants."

3 Which of the following is *not* included in a definition of a volcano?

 a. individual vents

 b. magma systems

 c. volcanic edifices

 d. volcanic fields

4 **Prose Constructed-Response** According to "On the Slopes of Mauna Loa, Hawaii Island," how can volcanic eruptions improve the natural landscape? Use details from at least two sources in your response.

_____

_____

_____

_____

5 **Prose Constructed-Response** Explain how the eruption of Mount Vesuvius affected the region around Naples. Cite text evidence in your response.

_____

_____

_____

_____

_____

_____

_____

_____

_____

6 **Prose Constructed-Response** Why is it important to define what a volcano is before discussing how many active volcanoes exist? Cite text evidence in your response.

_____

_____

_____

_____

_____

_____

_____

_____

_____

_____

Part 2: Write

ASSIGNMENT

You have read information about volcanoes. Write an informative essay examining how volcanoes affect people and environments. Include evidence from what you have read.

Plan

Use the graphic organizer to help you outline the structure of your informative essay.

Introduction and Cause

Effect and Supporting Details

Effect and Supporting Details

Effect and Supporting Details

Conclusion

© Houghton Mifflin Harcourt Publishing Company

Draft

 Use your notes and completed graphic organizer to write a first draft of your essay.

Revise and Edit

Look back over your essay and compare it to the Evaluation Criteria. Revise your essay and edit it to correct spelling, grammar, and punctuation errors.

Evaluation Criteria

Your teacher will be looking for:

1. Statement of purpose

▶ Is it clear what cause you are discussing, as well as its effects?

▶ Did you support the points with evidence?

2. Organization

▶ Are the sections of your essay organized in a logical way?

▶ Is there a smooth flow from beginning to end?

▶ Is there a clear conclusion that supports the thesis?

▶ Did you stay on topic?

3. Elaboration of evidence

▶ Is the evidence relevant to the topic?

▶ Is there enough evidence?

4. Conventions

▶ Did you follow the rules of grammar usage as well as punctuation, capitalization, and spelling?

Common Ground

Literary Analysis

© Houghton Mifflin Harcourt Publishing Company

STEP 1
ANALYZE THE MODEL

Evaluate the author's style in Nikki Giovanni's "Kidnap Poem."

STEP 2
PRACTICE THE TASK

Write an analysis of how the poem "The New Colossus" changed the way Americans view the Statue of Liberty.

STEP 3
PERFORM THE TASK

Write about how "The Charge of the Light Brigade" impacts your understanding of the events behind the poem.

Great literature has a profound effect on its audience. One reason for this is that good literature contains themes and ideas that are universal. We might read a story about a child from the eighteenth century or a warrior in a distant land and say to ourselves, "I've felt that way, too."

If themes and ideas about love, war, family, and friendship are common to different times and places, then what makes a work literary is the author's style. An author's style is *how* a work is written.

Style describes an author's word choice, sentence structure, figurative language, sentence length, and other aspects of writing. An author may choose a formal or an informal style, long or short sentences, easy or difficult vocabulary. Writers use these elements of style to emphasize ideas and create meaning.

IN THIS UNIT, you will analyze another student's response to a free-verse poem written by Nikki Giovanni. Then you will write a literary analysis of Emma Lazarus's famous poem "The New Colossus." Finally, you will analyze how "The Charge of the Light Brigade" affects your understanding of the events that inspired the poem.

How do authors use their own style to express common themes?

You will read:

▶ **A BIOGRAPHY**
Nikki Giovanni: The Poet and Her Craft

▶ **A POEM**
"Kidnap Poem"

You will analyze:

▶ **A STUDENT MODEL**
Nikki Giovanni's Unusual Style

Source Materials for Step 1

Ms. Golden assigned her class a poem by Nikki Giovanni to read and analyze. She also provided information about the poet. The notes in the side columns were written by Jocelyn, a student in Ms. Golden's class.

Nikki Giovanni: The Poet and Her Craft

The contemporary poet Nikki Giovanni was born in Knoxville, Tennessee, on June 7, 1943. She grew up in Lincoln Heights, Ohio, and attended Fisk University, later studying at the University of Pennsylvania and Columbia University. A noted African American poet and activist committed to the fight for civil rights and equality, Giovanni began writing in the turbulent period of the late 1960s. She credits both her poetry and her appreciation of her African American heritage to her grandmother, who was a gifted storyteller.

She seems proud of her heritage.

Giovanni's first books of poetry, published in 1968, grew out of her reaction to the assassinations of Martin Luther King Jr., Malcolm X, and Medgar Evers. After the birth of her son, Giovanni's work shifted to themes of family. In the 1970s, she began to write for both children and adults. Her children's books include *Ego-Tripping and Other Poems for Young People* (1973) and *Vacation Time* (1980). She wrote her noted memoir *Gemini* in 1971.

I can understand that.

Giovanni's early experience with the power of the spoken word had a deep influence on her style. Her poetry is informal, but rich with bright images. This informal style makes her accessible to children as well as adults. Giovanni is also notable for the unusual line breaks in her poetry. As readers pause at these line breaks, they experience everyday words and phrases in a fresh way.

This seems like a unique way of writing poetry.

Giovanni's keen ear for how people speak is at the core of her style. As a poet, she writes about the familiar in a way that captures the voice of real people.

Since 1987, she has been a professor of writing and literature.

Kidnap POEM

by Nikki Giovanni

ever been kidnapped
by a poet
if i were a poet
i'd kidnap you
put you in my phrases and meter
you to jones beach
or maybe coney island
or maybe just to my house
lyric you in lilacs
dash you in the rain
blend into the beach
to complement my see
play the lyre for you
ode you with my love song
anything to win you
wrap you in the red Black green
show you off to mama
yeah if i were a poet i'd kid
nap you

kidnapped by a poet, huh?

But she is a poet!

no capital letter for I? no punctuation? Why?

strange word choice—but sounds like music

Ode is usually a noun, not a verb.

She broke an everyday word into two words.

Discuss and Decide

With a partner, review Jocelyn's notes in the side column. What unique elements of the writer's style does she note? Cite text evidence in your discussion.

Analyze a Student Model for Step 1

Read Jocelyn's literary analysis closely. The red side notes are the comments that her teacher, Ms. Golden, wrote.

Jocelyn Anaya
Ms. Golden, English
February 2

Nikki Giovanni's Unusual Style

Jocelyn, great job in analyzing the poet's style in this poem!

Nikki Giovanni's "Kidnap Poem" asks the reader: "ever been kidnapped / by a poet"? Then she proceeds to "kidnap" the reader with her poem. In an informal, yet highly vivid poem, she tells what she would do for and to the person whom she loves.

As the speaker of the poem, Giovanni tells the reader that she would kidnap him or her, "if" she were a poet. The reader knows she is a poet and continues to read as Giovanni goes on to prove the fact. She takes the reader to "jones beach" and "coney island" or, upon reflection, home with her. She would even wrap the reader in the African "red Black green" flag.

Breaking the rules is an important concept in her poetry.

Nice discussion.

Giovanni breaks a lot of rules in the poem. In her poetry, capitalization and punctuation are entirely up to the poet. She creates new words and grammar for her poem. The noun "meter" becomes a verb as she "meters" her "victim" to poetic places, perhaps by taxi. She also "lyrics" her love object "in lilacs." This word choice is informal, but it is new and colorful.

Tell me more about her informal style. How is it different from other poetry?

Giovanni's informal tone creates a feeling of closeness that is appropriate for a love poem. Her style, with peaks and unusual line breaks, expresses the excitement she feels at actually wanting to kidnap the "you" in the poem. Her line breaks, in the middle of a thought—and even in the middle of a word—convey a breathlessness ("i'd kid / nap you") about the poet's love.

1. Analyze   2. Practice   3. Perform

The images of Coney Island and lilacs jump out at the reader and appeal to the senses. Giovanni uses the first-person ("I") point of view and addresses the "you" of the poem in an intimate way. Overall, the poem is personal.

I like the analysis of the poem and how the poet relates to her ideas about love.

Use the last line to develop a strong conclusion.

Great job, Jocelyn!

Discuss and Decide

With a partner, discuss the way the unique aspects of Giovanni's style affect Jocelyn's interpretation of the poem. Cite text evidence in your discussion.

Terminology of Literary Analysis

Read each word and explanation. Then look back at Jocelyn's literary analysis and find an example to complete the chart.

Term	Explanation	Example from Jocelyn's Essay
theme	The **theme** is the underlying message about life or human nature that the writer wants the reader to understand.	
style	The **style** is the particular way in which a work of literature is written—not *what* is said but *how* it is said.	
tone	The **tone** is the attitude the writer takes toward a subject.	
figurative language	**Figurative language** is language used in an imaginative way to convey ideas that are not literally true.	
voice	The **voice** is a writer's unique use of language that allows a reader to "hear" a human personality in the writer's work.	
diction	**Diction** is the writer's choice of words. Diction can make a work sound formal or informal, serious or humorous.	
imagery	**Imagery** consists of words and phrases that appeal to the senses.	

1. Analyze   2. Practice   3. Perform

How can poetry create common ground?

You will read:

▶ **A POEM**
"The New Colossus"

▶ **A NEWSPAPER ARTICLE**
"How a Sonnet Turned a Statue into the 'Mother of Exiles'"

You will write:

▶ **A LITERARY ANALYSIS**
How does "The New Colossus" affect the way we view the Statue of Liberty?

Source Materials for Step 2

AS YOU READ You will be writing a literary analysis that answers the question: How does "The New Colossus" affect the way we view the Statue of Liberty? Carefully study the sources in Step 2. As you read, underline and circle information that may be useful to you when you write your essay.

Source 1: Poem

The New Colossus

by Emma Lazarus

Not like the brazen giant of Greek fame,
With conquering limbs astride from land to land;
Here at our sea-washed, sunset gates shall stand
A mighty woman with a torch, whose flame
5 Is the imprisoned lightning, and her name
Mother of Exiles. From her beacon-hand
Glows world-wide welcome; her mild eyes command
The air-bridged harbor that twin cities frame.
"Keep, ancient lands, your storied pomp!" cries she
10 With silent lips. "Give me your tired, your poor,
Your huddled masses yearning to breathe free,
The wretched refuse of your teeming shore.
Send these, the homeless, tempest-tost to me.
I lift my lamp beside the golden door!"

Close Read

Reread lines 10–14. How do these words convey the idea that the statue is the "Mother of Exiles" (line 6)? Support your reasons with specific evidence from the text.

_____

_____

Source 2: Newspaper Article

THE NEW YORK TIMES   THURSDAY, OCTOBER 27, 2011

HOW A SONNET TURNED A STATUE INTO THE "MOTHER OF EXILES"

by Sam Roberts

When the Goddess of Liberty was given to the United States, its donor's agenda was to burnish France's republican roots after the oppressive reign of Napoleon III and to celebrate the two nations' commitment to the principles of liberty.

The only immigrants mentioned at the dedication in 1886 were the "illustrious descendants of the French nobility" who
10 fought on behalf of the United States against Britain during the American Revolution.

But it was the words of a fourth-generation American whose father was a wealthy sugar refiner and whose great-great-uncle welcomed George Washington to Newport, R.I., that almost single-handedly transformed the monumental statue in New York Harbor into the "Mother of Exiles" that would symbolically beckon generations of
20 immigrants.

Emma Lazarus's poem only belatedly became synonymous with the Statue of

Liberty, whose 125th birthday as a gift from France will be celebrated Friday by the National Park Service.

Lazarus's "New Colossus," with its memorable appeal to "give me your tired, your poor," was commissioned for a fundraising campaign by artists and writers to pay for the statue's pedestal.

But while the poem was critically acclaimed, it was not even mentioned at the dedication ceremony.

Finally in 1903, after relentless lobbying by a friend of Lazarus who was descended from Alexander Hamilton, himself an immigrant, it was "affixed to the pedestal as an ex post facto inscription," the art historian Marvin Trachtenberg wrote.

"Gradually, thereafter, the awareness spread not only of the significance of the lines of the poem but also of the significance of the aspect of national tradition it expressed," another historian, Oscar Handlin, wrote. "Liberty was not simply the bond between ancient allies; nor was it only the symbol of liberal ideas of justice and freedom; it was also the motive force that had peopled the wilderness and made the country that emerged what it was."

Barry Moreno, a historian of the statue for the Park Service, recalled that it "was never built for immigrants."

"It was," he recalled, "built to pay tribute to the United States of America, the Declaration of Independence, American democracy and democracy throughout the world. It honored the end of slavery, honored the end of all sorts of tyranny and also friendship between France and America."

Only later, he said, "letters were written home, word of mouth, taught people that you would see this wonderful goddess in New York Harbor when you arrived in America to welcome you."

"And it was really immigrants that lifted her up to a sort of a glory that was probably before America really fully embraced her," he added.

Lazarus, who popularized that "wonderful goddess," accepted the commission only begrudgingly—few poets relish the idea of writing on demand. But she was stirred by a wave of pogroms against Jews in Russia and by her regular visits to poor immigrants housed in temporary shelters on Wards Island. She would make "The New Colossus" the first entry in a compendium of poems she anthologized shortly before her death from Hodgkin's disease at 38 in 1887.

The poem went unmentioned in her obituary in *The New York Times*, but it appeared in a brief article in 1903 when the plaque was dedicated. (An exhibition on Lazarus, the "Poet of Exiles," opened Wednesday at the Museum of Jewish Heritage in Lower Manhattan. A manuscript of the poem is at the Center for Jewish History.)

"Emma Lazarus was the first American to make any sense of this statue," said Esther Schor, an English professor at Princeton and author of a biography titled *Emma Lazarus*.

Professor Schor said that the statue, conceived by the French statesman Édouard René de Laboulaye, "was to propound the values of the French Revolution, in a sort of end-run around the repressive Second Empire of Napoleon III."

"But," she continued, "Americans were so unmoved and uninterested that it was hard to raise money simply to build a pedestal to support it."

For Lazarus, who wrote the sonnet in 1883 having seen only the torch when it was on display for a fund-raising drive in Madison Square Park, "it was a moment of moral and spiritual recovery, after her attempts to raise money to benefit the Russian-Jewish refugees of 1881–82 had largely fallen on deaf ears," Professor Schor said.

Instead of retreating, Professor Schor said, she broadened her appeal to all immigrants. For her "the statue was a special kind of mother—a 'mother of exiles'—a mother whose mission is not to reproduce herself, but rather to adopt the abandoned, the orphaned, the persecuted," she said.

The sonnet would survive periodic efforts to excise her reference to "wretched refuse" and would become enshrined in the political lexicon in the 1930s as an anthem for Americans who, with war again threatening in Europe, lobbied to reverse anti-immigration quotas that had been imposed a decade earlier.

"The irony is that the statue goes on speaking, even when the tide turns against immigration—even against immigrants themselves, as they adjust to their American lives," Professor Schor said. "You can't think of the statue without hearing the words Emma Lazarus gave her."

Discuss and Decide

With a small group, talk about whether the newspaper article is effective in explaining the historical events surrounding the poem. Cite specific evidence from the text in your discussion.

Respond to Questions on Step 2 Sources

These questions will help you analyze the sources you've read. Use your notes and refer to the sources in order to answer the questions. Your answers to these questions will help you write your essay.

1 Which of the following best describes the relationship between Emma Lazarus's poem and the history surrounding the Statue of Liberty?

   a. The statue became a symbol of hope for immigrants after the poem was written.

   b. The poet wrote the poem at the time of France's gift of the statue to the United States.

   c. The Statue of Liberty was built to encourage immigrants to come to the United States.

   d. The poem celebrates the love of democracy that the United States and France share.

2 Select the three pieces of evidence from Lazarus's poem and the newspaper article that best support your answer to Question 1.

   a. "Not like the brazen giant of Greek fame, / With conquering limbs . . ." ("The New Colossus," lines 1–2)

   b. "A mighty woman with a torch, whose flame / Is the imprisoned lightning . . ." ("The New Colossus," lines 4–5)

   c. " . . . her mild eyes command / The air-bridged harbor that twin cities frame." ("The New Colossus," lines 7–8)

   d. "'Give me your tired, your poor, / Your huddled masses yearning to breathe free . . .'" ("The New Colossus," lines 10–11)

   e. "But it was the words of a fourth-generation American . . . that almost single-handedly transformed the monumental statue in New York Harbor into the 'Mother of Exiles' that would symbolically beckon generations of immigrants." ("How a Sonnet," lines 12–20)

   f. "Emma Lazarus's poem only belatedly became synonymous with the Statute of Liberty . . ." ("How a Sonnet," lines 21–23)

   g. "The poem went unmentioned in her obituary in *The New York Times*, but it appeared in a brief article in 1903 when the plaque was dedicated." ("How a Sonnet," lines 81–84)

   h. "For her 'the statue was . . . a mother whose mission is not to reproduce herself, but rather to adopt the abandoned, the orphaned, the persecuted . . .'" ("How a Sonnet," lines 115–119)

3 What does the article reveal about the poem and its significance to the people of the United States?

   a. The poem was actually used by people who opposed immigration to the United States.

   b. The poem was originally written to foster immigration to the United States.

   c. The poem linked the statue and immigration; it was not the original meaning of the statue.

   d. The poem was originally written to honor another statue given by France to the United States.

4 Select the three pieces of evidence from Lazarus's sonnet and the newspaper article that best support your answer to Question 3.

   a. "Not like the brazen giant of Greek fame, / With conquering limbs . . ." ("The New Colossus," lines 1–2)

   b. "Here at our sea-washed, sunset gates shall stand / A mighty woman with a torch . . ." ("The New Colossus," lines 3–4)

   c. " . . . her mild eyes command / The air-bridged harbor that twin cities frame." ("The New Colossus," lines 7–8)

   d. "'Send these, the homeless, tempest-tossed to me.'" ("The New Colossus," line 13)

   e. "Emma Lazarus's poem only belatedly became synonymous with the Statute of Liberty . . ." ("How a Sonnet," lines 21–23)

   f. "The poem went unmentioned in her obituary in *The New York Times* . . ." ("How a Sonnet," lines 81–82)

   g. " . . . conceived by the French statesman Édouard René de Laboulaye, [the statue] 'was to propound the values of the French Revolution . . .'" ("How a Sonnet," lines 96–98)

   h. "'The irony is that the statue goes on speaking, even when the tide turns against immigration—even against immigrants themselves, as they adjust to their American lives . . .'" ("How a Sonnet," lines 128–132)

5 **Prose Constructed-Response** What events inspired Emma Lazarus to write her poem? Cite evidence from the newspaper article.

_____

_____

_____

_____

6 **Prose Constructed-Response** What was the initial reaction of the people of the United States to the Statue of Liberty? How did Emma Lazarus's poem change the way the statue was viewed? Cite evidence from the poem and the newspaper article.

_____

_____

_____

_____

7 **Prose Constructed-Response** How does the Statue of Liberty "go on speaking" to immigrants today? Cite evidence from the poem and the newspaper article.

_____

_____

_____

_____

Planning and Prewriting

Analyze the Sources

You have read Emma Lazarus's poem "The New Colossus" and the newspaper article "How a Sonnet Turned a Statue Into the 'Mother of Exiles.'" Think about how the information in these two sources helped you understand how Lazarus's poem affected the way we view the Statue of Liberty.

In order to write this literary analysis, think about how you will explain the reasons behind a particular event. Sometimes multiple causes contribute to one event (or effect). Other times, a single cause can lead to multiple outcomes. In still other situations, one event triggers the next event to occur, which causes another event to happen in a causal chain of events. Consider which pattern of organization works best for this topic.

You may prefer to do your planning on a computer.

Decide on Key Points

Think about the key points and relationships you will include in your essay. As you make notes, identify the connection between the poem and the real events that occurred as a result. Use specific evidence from the poem and *The New York Times* article to list your key points.

Point 1	Point 2	Point 3

Organizing Your Essay

Before you begin to write your literary analysis, decide how you want to organize it. Determine whether you are looking for one cause and multiple effects, multiple causes and one effect, or a causal chain of causes and effects—how each event in a series caused another event to happen. For each of the three organizational strategies below, your essay will begin with an introductory paragraph and end with a concluding paragraph.

1. Single Cause/Multiple Effects

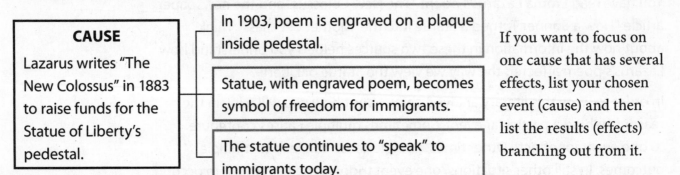

CAUSE

Lazarus writes "The New Colossus" in 1883 to raise funds for the Statue of Liberty's pedestal.

In 1903, poem is engraved on a plaque inside pedestal.

Statue, with engraved poem, becomes symbol of freedom for immigrants.

The statue continues to "speak" to immigrants today.

If you want to focus on one cause that has several effects, list your chosen event (cause) and then list the results (effects) branching out from it.

2. Multiple Causes/Single Effect

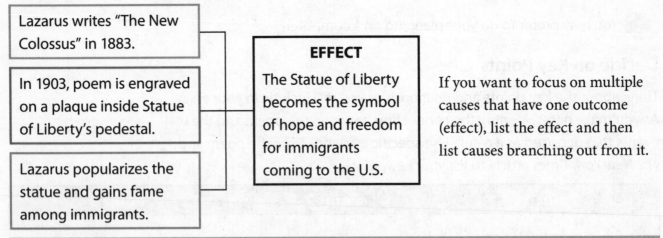

Lazarus writes "The New Colossus" in 1883.

In 1903, poem is engraved on a plaque inside Statue of Liberty's pedestal.

Lazarus popularizes the statue and gains fame among immigrants.

EFFECT

The Statue of Liberty becomes the symbol of hope and freedom for immigrants coming to the U.S.

If you want to focus on multiple causes that have one outcome (effect), list the effect and then list causes branching out from it.

3. Causal Chain

In a causal chain, one event causes the next event to happen. The second event causes the third event, which causes the fourth event to occur.

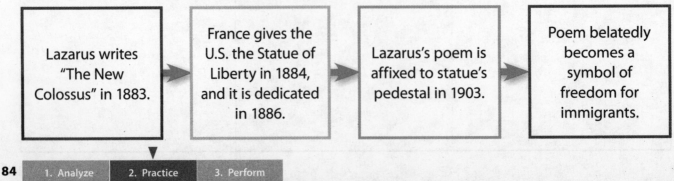

Lazarus writes "The New Colossus" in 1883.

France gives the U.S. the Statue of Liberty in 1884, and it is dedicated in 1886.

Lazarus's poem is affixed to statue's pedestal in 1903.

Poem belatedly becomes a symbol of freedom for immigrants.

Draft Your Essay

As you write, think about:

▶ **Audience:** Your teacher

▶ **Purpose:** Demonstrate your understanding of the specific requirements of a literary analysis.

▶ **Style:** Use a formal and objective tone.

▶ **Transitions:** Use words and phrases such as *consequently, because, since,* and *as a result* to show cause and effect.

Revise

Revision Checklist: Self Evaluation

Use the checklist below to guide your analysis.

 If you drafted your essay on the computer, you may wish to print it out so that you can more easily evaluate it.

Ask Yourself	Tips	Revision Strategies
1. Does the introduction grab the audience's attention and include a main idea?	Draw a line under the attention-getting text. Circle the main idea.	Add a sentence, question, observation, or historical fact. Make your main idea clear.
2. Is the relationship a true cause-and-effect relationship, and is it supported by textual evidence?	Underline each example that indicates a cause and its effect. Circle the evidence from the text and draw a line to the relationship it supports.	Add examples or revise existing ones to show true cause-and-effect connections. Provide explicit evidence from the text.
3. Are appropriate connections made between each cause and effect, and are varied transitions used to make connections clearer?	Place a checkmark next to each transitional word or phrase. Add transitional words or phrases where needed to organize or clarify cause-and-effect relationships.	Add transitional words and phrases to clarify the connection between a cause and its effect.
4. Is there a strong conclusion that follows from or is supported by the preceding paragraphs?	Put a double underscore under the concluding statement. Star the text that supports or builds up to the conclusion. Underline the insight offered to readers.	Add an overarching view of key points or a final observation about the significance of the cause and effect.

Revision Checklist: Peer Review

Exchange your essay with a classmate, or read it aloud to your partner. As you read and comment on your classmate's essay, focus on logic, organization, and evidence—not on whether you agree with the author's claim. Help each other identify parts of the draft that need strengthening, reworking, or a new approach.

What To Look For	Notes for My Partner
1. Does the introduction grab the audience's attention and include a controlling idea?	
2. Is there specific textual evidence to support your key points?	
3. Are appropriate and varied transitions used to show relationships between each cause and effect?	
4. Is there a strong conclusion that follows from or is supported by the preceding paragraphs? Does it leave the reader with something to think about?	

Edit

Edit your essay to correct spelling, grammar, and punctuation errors.

How do we respond to historic events?

You will read:

▶ **AN EYEWITNESS ACCOUNT**
The Battle of Balaclava

▶ **AN INFORMATIONAL TEXT**
Narrative Poems

▶ **A NARRATIVE POEM**
"The Charge of the Light Brigade"

You will write:

▶ **A LITERARY ANALYSIS**
How does "The Charge of the Light Brigade" by Alfred, Lord Tennyson affect your understanding of the real events behind the poem?

Part 1: Read Sources

Source 1: Eyewitness Account

The Battle of Balaclava

AS YOU READ *Pay attention to the details and historical facts in this newspaper article, written by William Howard Russell on October 25, 1854. Note how this eyewitness account of the charge of the Light Brigade during the Battle of Balaclava lends historical accuracy and meaning to Alfred, Lord Tennyson's poem. Record comments or questions about the text in the side margins.*

NOTES

Background

Although the Crimean War, which erupted in 1853 with the Russian Empire on one side and Britain, France, the Kingdom of Sardinia, and the Ottoman Empire on the other is now only a dim memory, what is remembered is one tragic battle of the war—the brave cavalry charge of the British Light Brigade into Russian fire—an action made famous by Alfred, Lord Tennyson's poem. Through a miscommunication of orders, the Light Brigade of about 600 horsemen began a headlong charge into a valley near the city of Balaclava, in the Crimea, on October 25, 1854, with the idea of capturing some Russian artillery. Unknown to the cavalry, the valley was surrounded by Russian troops on three sides, and an estimated 278 of the British Light Brigade were killed or wounded.

When news of the disaster hit London by way of the newspaper account of the charge written by William Howard Russell, the first true foreign correspondent, it caused a national scandal that prompted Tennyson to write his poem. An eyewitness to the battle, here is Russell's account for the London Times as the Light Brigade begins its charge into "the valley of Death."

1. Analyze   2. Practice   3. Perform

The Battle Of Balaclava

The Times, 14 November 1854
reported by William Howard Russell

They swept proudly past, glittering in the morning sun in
all the pride and splendour of war. We could hardly believe
the evidence of our senses! Surely that handful of men were
not going to charge an army in position? Alas! it was but too
true—their desperate valour knew no bounds, and far indeed
was it removed from its so-called better part—discretion.
They advanced in two lines, quickening their pace as they
closed towards the enemy. A more fearful spectacle was never
witnessed than by those who, without the power to aid, beheld

10   their heroic countrymen rushing to the arms of death. At the
distance of 1200 yards the whole line of the enemy belched
forth, from thirty iron mouths, a flood of smoke and flame,
through which hissed the deadly balls. Their flight was marked
by instant gaps in our ranks, by dead men and horses, by steeds
flying wounded or riderless across the plain. The first line
was broken—it was joined by the second, they never halted
or checked their speed an instant. With diminished ranks,
thinned by those thirty guns, which the Russians had laid with
the most deadly accuracy, with a halo of flashing steel above

20   their heads, and with a cheer which was many a noble fellow's
death cry, they flew into the smoke of the batteries; but ere they
were lost from view, the plain was strewed with their bodies
and with the carcasses of horses. They were exposed to an
oblique fire from the batteries on the hills on both sides, as well
as to a direct fire of musketry.

Through the clouds of smoke we could see their sabres
flashing as they rode up to the guns and dashed between them,
cutting down the gunners as they stood. . . . We saw them
riding through the guns, as I have said; to our delight we saw

30   them returning, after breaking through a column of Russian

infantry, and scattering them like chaff, when the flank fire of the battery on the hill swept them down, scattered and broken as they were. Wounded men and dismounted troopers flying towards us told the sad tale. . . . At the very moment when they were about to retreat, an enormous mass of lancers was hurled upon their flank. Colonel Shewell, of the 8th Hussars, saw the danger, and rode his few men straight at them, cutting his way through with fearful loss. The other regiments turned and engaged in a desperate encounter. With courage too great

40 almost for credence, they were breaking their way through the columns which enveloped them, when there took place an act of atrocity without parallel in the modem warfare of civilized nations. The Russian gunners, when the storm of cavalry passed, returned to their guns. They saw their own cavalry mingled with the troopers who had just ridden over them, and to the eternal disgrace of the Russian name the miscreants poured a murderous volley of grape and canister on the mass of struggling men and horses, mingling friend and foe in one common ruin. It was as much as our Heavy Cavalry Brigade

50 could do to cover the retreat of the miserable remnants of that band of heroes as they returned to the place they had so lately quitted in all the pride of life.

At twenty-five to twelve not a British soldier, except the dead and dying, was left in front of these bloody Muscovite guns.

Close Read

Reread lines 1–10. How does Russell's account use descriptive details and figurative language to portray the cavalrymen about to charge? Cite specific evidence from the text in your response.

_____

_____

_____

_____

1. Analyze   2. Practice   3. Perform

Narrative Poems

by Amelia Johnson

A narrative poem is a poem that tells a story. Narrative poetry was originally inspired by traditional epics and ballads, which are long poems that also tell a story. These epics and ballads were often based on actual events. However, these events are presented in a way that makes them seem larger than life.

Because a narrative poem tells a story, it emphasizes plot and action, much as a prose short story or a novel would. The setting and the characters' reactions are also important elements. However, it also contains poetic techniques such as
10 rhythm and rhyme that are found in other forms of poetry.

In the nineteenth century, narrative poetry was very popular in the United States and in Europe. Henry Wadsworth Longfellow, the most famous American poet of his day, wrote numerous poems that told a story. Many of them, including "Paul Revere's Ride," were based on true events. However, the poems did not always depict those events with absolute historical accuracy.

Newspapers also were available to greater numbers of people during this time, and they became a source of subject
20 matter for narrative poems. In the case of "The Charge of the Light Brigade," Alfred, Lord Tennyson, the well-known British poet, was inspired to write his poem by the news reporting of William Howard Russell, the first modern foreign correspondent to witness and report on the actual events of a

© Houghton Mifflin Harcourt Publishing Company • Image Credits: ©Fotolia

AS YOU READ *Focus on the aspects of narrative poetry that make it different from other kinds of poetry. Record comments or questions about the text in the side margins.*

NOTES

war. Russell's dramatic eyewitness accounts of the Crimean War, which he wrote for *The London Illustrated News,* were also printed in *The Times.* His dispatches were read by so many people that the events of the charge of the Light Brigade and the tragic death of so many British cavalry caused a national
30 scandal in Britain. Both Russell's eyewitness account and Tennyson's poem captured the tragedy of the doomed charge.

However, the way the newspaper article and the poem present these events is very different. Tennyson's narrative poem includes elements that are found in short stories such as plot, characters, and setting. In addition, Tennyson includes these poetic techniques:

- Rhythm is the pattern of stressed and unstressed syllables in a line of poetry.

- Rhyme is the repetition of sounds at the ends of words.

40 • Repetition is the use of a word, phrase, or line more than once.

As you read Tennyson's poem, look for these elements of narrative poetry and the effect they create.

Discuss and Decide

Think about the characteristics of a narrative poem described in the text. Why might a military battle be a good topic for a narrative poem? Cite text evidence in your discussion.

1. Analyze   2. Practice   3. Perform

The Charge of the Light Brigade

by Alfred, Lord Tennyson

Half a league, half a league,
    Half a league onward,
All in the valley of Death
    Rode the six hundred.
5 "Forward, the Light Brigade!
Charge for the guns!" he said:
Into the valley of Death
    Rode the six hundred.

"Forward, the Light Brigade!"
10 Was there a man dismay'd?
Not tho' the soldier knew
    Some one had blunder'd:
Theirs not to make reply,
Theirs not to reason why,
15 Theirs but to do and die:
Into the valley of Death
    Rode the six hundred.

AS YOU READ *Note the features of narrative poetry that the poem contains. Be aware of the similarities and differences between the poem and William Howard Russell's eyewitness account. Underline details that contribute to your understanding of the narrative text and reflect the facts behind the poem. Record comments or questions in the side margins.*

NOTES

Cannon to right of them,
Cannon to left of them,
20 Cannon in front of them
    Volley'd and thunder'd;
Storm'd at with shot and shell,
Boldly they rode and well,
Into the jaws of Death,
25 Into the mouth of Hell
    Rode the six hundred.

Flash'd all their sabers bare,
Flash'd as they turn'd in air,
Sabring the gunners there,
30 Charging an army, while
    All the world wonder'd:
Plunged in the battery smoke
Right thro' the line they broke;
Cossack and Russian
35 Reel'd from the saber-stroke
    Shatter'd and sunder'd.
Then they rode back, but not,
    Not the six hundred.

Close Read

Reread lines 1–26. Note the use of repetition in these lines. What ideas do these repeated phrases emphasize? Cite specific text evidence in your response.

_____

_____

_____

1. Analyze 2. Practice 3. Perform

Cannon to right of them,
40 Cannon to left of them,
Cannon behind them
    Volley'd and thunder'd;
Storm'd at with shot and shell,
While horse and hero fell,
45 They that had fought so well
Came thro' the jaws of Death,
Back from the mouth of Hell,
All that was left of them,
    Left of six hundred.

50 When can their glory fade?
O the wild charge they made!
    All the world wonder'd.
Honor the charge they made!
Honor the Light Brigade,
55   Noble six hundred!

Discuss and Decide

With a small group, discuss which specific details are in both the eyewitness account and the narrative poem. Why might these details have been included by both writers? Cite specific text evidence in your discussion.

Respond to Questions on Step 3 Sources

These questions will help you think about the texts you have read. Use your notes and refer to the sources in order to answer the questions. Your answers to these questions will help you write your literary analysis.

1 **Prose Constructed-Response** A plot is a feature of all narrative poems. Summarize the plot of "The Charge of the Light Brigade."

_____

_____

_____

_____

2 **Prose Constructed-Response** How does the use of rhyme and repetition contribute to the meaning of the poem? What ideas are emphasized? Cite text evidence in your response.

_____

_____

_____

_____

_____

3 **Prose Constructed-Response** What are the historical facts of "The Battle of Balaclava" and "The Charge of the Light Brigade"? How are they similar? What are the differences? Cite specific evidence from the two texts.

_____

_____

_____

_____

Part 2: Write

ASSIGNMENT

Write a literary analysis that answers the question: How does "The Charge of the Light Brigade" by Alfred, Lord Tennyson affect your understanding of the real events behind the poem?

Plan

Use the graphic organizer to help you organize your literary analysis.

Introduction

Key Point 1

Key Point 2

Key Point 3

Conclusion

Draft

 Use your notes and completed graphic organizer to write a first draft of your literary analysis.

Revise and Edit

 Look back over your essay and compare it to the Evaluation Criteria. Revise your literary analysis and edit it to correct spelling, grammar, and punctuation errors.

Evaluation Criteria

Your teacher will be looking for:

1. *Statement of purpose*

▶ Did you clearly state your controlling idea?

▶ Did you respond to the assignment question?

▶ Did you support it with valid reasons?

2. *Organization*

▶ Are the sections of your literary analysis organized in a logical way?

▶ Is there a smooth flow from beginning to end?

▶ Is there a clear conclusion that supports your controlling idea?

▶ Did you stay on topic?

3. *Elaboration of evidence*

▶ Did you cite evidence from the sources, and is it relevant to the topic?

▶ Is there sufficient evidence?

4. *Language and vocabulary*

▶ Did you use a formal, essay-appropriate tone?

▶ Did you use vocabulary familiar to your audience?

5. *Conventions*

▶ Did you follow the rules of grammar usage as well as punctuation, capitalization, and spelling?

On Your Own

TASK 1

RESEARCH SIMULATION

Argumentative Essay

Your school debate team has a competition coming up, and you have been assigned the topic of child labor in the modern world. To prepare for the debate, you will write an argumentative essay.

First you will review three articles on child labor. After you have reviewed these sources, you will answer some questions about them. You should first skim the sources and questions, and then go back and read them carefully.

In Part 2, you will write an argumentative essay about whether you agree or disagree that it is okay to buy products that have been manufactured using child labor.

Time Management: Argumentative Task

There are two parts to most formal writing tests. Both parts of the tests are timed, so it's important to use your limited time wisely.

Part 1: Read Sources and Answer Questions

Preview the Assignment

35 minutes

35 minutes! That's not much time.

You will have 35 minutes to read the sources and decide whether you agree or disagree that it is okay to buy products manufactured with the use of child labor. You will also answer questions that will help you plan your essay on the topic.

Preview the questions. This will help you know which information you'll need to find as you read.

How Many?

How many pages of reading?

How many multiple-choice questions?

How many prose constructed-response questions?

Underline, circle, and take notes as you read. You probably won't have time to reread.

How do you plan to use the 35 minutes?

This is a lot to do in a short time.

Estimated time to read:

Source #1: "Nike Pledges to End Child Labor and Apply U.S. Rules Abroad"   minutes

Source #2: "Nike's Dilemma: Is Doing the Right Thing Wrong?"   minutes

Source #3: "This Company Is Employing Children?"   minutes

Estimated time to answer questions?   minutes

Total   **35   minutes**

Any concerns?

_____

Part 2: Write the Essay

70

Plan and Write an Argumentative Essay

70 minutes

You will have 70 minutes to plan, write, revise, and edit your essay.

Your Plan

Before you start to write, decide on your precise claim and reasons. Then think about the evidence you will use to support your reasons.

How do you plan to use the 70 minutes?

Estimated time for planning the essay?		minutes
Estimated time for writing?		minutes
Estimated time for editing?		minutes
Estimated time for checking spelling, grammar, and punctuation?		minutes
Total	**70**	**minutes**

Notes:

_____

_____

_____

_____

How much time do you have? Pay attention to the clock.

Be sure to leave enough time for this step.

Reread your essay, making sure that the points are clear. Check that there are no spelling or punctuation mistakes.

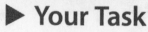 **Your Task**

> Your debate team is preparing for a competition. You
> are to write an argumentative essay on whether it is
> okay to buy products made with the use of child labor.
> In researching the topic, you have identified three
> sources you will use in planning your argumentative
> essay.

After you have reviewed the sources, you will answer some questions
about them. Briefly skim the sources and the three questions that
follow. Then, go back and read the sources carefully so you will have the
information you will need to answer the questions. Take notes on the
sources as you read. You may refer back to your notes at any time during
Part 1 or Part 2 of the performance task.

▶ Part 1 (35 minutes)

You will now read the sources. After carefully reading the sources, use
the rest of the time in Part 1 to answer the three questions about them.
Though your answers to these questions will help you think about what
you have read and plan your essay, they will also be scored as part of
the test.

SOURCE #1:
INTERNATIONAL BUSINESS

Nike Pledges to End Child Labor And Apply U.S. Rules Abroad

by John H. Cushman, Jr.
The New York Times   *May 13, 1998*

Bowing to pressure from critics who have tried to turn its famous shoe brand into a synonym for exploitation, Nike Inc. promised today to root out underage workers and require overseas manufacturers of its wares to meet strict United States health and safety standards.

Philip H. Knight, Nike's chairman and chief executive, also agreed to a demand that the company has long resisted, pledging to allow outsiders from labor and human rights groups to join the independent auditors who inspect the
10 factories in Asia, interviewing workers and assessing working conditions.

"We believe that these are practices which the conscientious, good companies will follow in the 21st century," he said in a speech here at the National Press Club. "These moves do more than just set industry standards. They reflect who we are as a company."

Nike said it would raise the minimum age for hiring new workers at shoe factories to 18 and the minimum for new workers at other plants to 16, in countries where it is common
20 for 14-year-olds to hold such jobs. It will not require the dismissal of underage workers already in place.

Footwear factories have heavier machinery and use more dangerous raw material, including solvents that cause toxic air pollution. At overseas factories that produce Nike shoes, the company said, it would tighten air-quality controls to insure that the air breathed by workers meets the same standards enforced by the United States Occupational Safety and Health Administration at home.

30 Mr. Knight's pledges did not include increased wage, a major complaint of critics who say that Nike and other American companies pay workers in China and Vietnam less than $2 a day and workers in Indonesia less than $1 a day. (A 1996 World Bank report concluded that more than one-fifth of the world's population lives on less than $1 a day.) Still, even with much lower prices in these countries, critics say workers need to make at least $3 a day to achieve adequate living standards.

Nike, in a statement today, cited a report it commissioned in 1997, which said that its factories in Indonesia and Vietnam 40 pay legal minimum wages and more.

In his speech today, Mr. Knight defended Nike's record of creating jobs and improving factory conditions abroad, but seemed to acknowledge that it was time for drastic action. "The Nike product has become synonymous with slave wages, forced overtime and arbitrary abuse," he said. "I truly believe that the American consumer does not want to buy products made in abusive conditions."

Jeffrey D. Ballinger, director of Press for Change, a group that has been critical of Nike, called the company's plan a major 50 retreat and a sign of the critics' growing strength.

The company has been hurt by falling stock prices and weak sales even as it has been pummeled in the public relations arena.

Mr. Knight said the main causes of the company's falling sales were the financial crisis in Asia, where the company had been expanding sales aggressively, and its failure to recognize a shifting consumer preference for hiking shoes.

"I truthfully don't think that there has been a material impact on Nike sales by the human rights attacks," he said, 60 citing the company's marketing studies.

But for months, the company, which spends huge sums for advertising and endorsements by big-name athletes, has responded increasingly forcefully to complaints about its employment practices, as student groups have demanded that universities doing business with Nike hold it to higher standards.

Mr. Knight emphasized today that using objective observers to monitor working conditions would serve not just Nike, but eventually American industry in general, by "giving the American consumer an assurance that those products are made under good conditions."

Some critics, though, stressed that the company could not reassure consumers without improving wages in its factories.

"We see one big gap," said Medea Benjamin, director of the San Francisco-based human rights group Global Exchange. "A sweatshop is a sweatshop is a sweatshop unless you start paying a living wage. That would be $3 a day."

Am I on Track?

Actual Time Spent Reading

Is Doing the Right Thing Wrong?

A child labor dispute could eliminate 4,000 Pakistani jobs.

by David Montero
Christian Science Monitor

December 22, 2006

NOTES

SIALKOT, PAKISTAN

In this bustling commercial hub near the Kashmiri border, fortunes seem to rise and fall with the Nike swoosh. Some 80 percent of the world's soccer balls are produced here by Nike and other top sports brands—making Sialkot, a city of 3 million, a model of prosperity in a country where poverty and extremism freely intermingle.

But there is a controversy behind this pot of gold. In November, Nike severed its contract with Saga Sports, its chief supplier, saying Saga's poor management exposes Nike to the
10 threat of child labor and other labor violations.

The incident, observers say, highlights the moral dilemma of first-world corporations using third-world labor. And since it is Pakistan, the outcome may be more pressing than elsewhere in the world.

Many say a surge of unemployment and falling profits in Sialkot, a rare oasis, is the last thing a Pakistan struggling with militant Islam and poverty needs.

A soul-searching debate is now coursing through the country: Child labor is universally condemned, but is it fair for
20 multinationals[1] to cut and run when incidents arise of children working? Or do corporations have an obligation to work to fix these problems themselves?

For Nike's part, the Beaverton, Oregon-based firm stated in a November press release that it will continue working with contract factories in China and Thailand to supply hand-stitched balls. Nike's contracts with Saga will expire in March.

---

[1] **multinationals:** businesses that have companies in more than one country

About Saga's 5,000 stitchers, it added: "[I]n this case, the company exhausted all options and was left with no alternative but to cease orders, despite the potential impact to workers and
30 the near-term effect on Nike's soccer ball business."

Gloomy-looking executives at Saga Sports, 70 percent of whose work is for Nike, say they're confident they can keep the company on board. The US Embassy recently told the Sialkot Chamber of Commerce that Nike will continue its other textile operations with existing contractors in Pakistan, according to unofficial statements from American officials.

By severing its contract with Saga, Nike is likely to score moral points with its customers in the West. But it's also likely, observers agree, to sink Saga, a corporate giant that makes about 6 million
40 of Pakistan's annual production of 40-million soccer balls.

Saga estimates that as many as 20,000 families could be affected, since 70 percent of the local market relies on them for work.

"Definitely, Saga did wrong. But does the wrong they did warrant Nike leaving?" asks Nasir Dogar, chief executive of the Independent Monitoring Association for Child Labor (IMAC), which oversees compliance at Sialkot's 3,000 soccer-ball stitching centers.

Sialkot's hand-stitched ball industry, about a century old, is
50 big business: Saga Sports alone accounted for $33 million of the industry's $210 million total. For Sialkot's 45,000 stitchers, who earn less than $100 a month on average, soccer balls are a way of life.

But for as long as there have been soccer balls in Sialkot, the hands of children have stitched them. That is not unusual in Pakistan, where a per capita income of about $2,800 commonly drives children to work. According to UNICEF estimates, more than 3 million boys and girls below age 14 work in Pakistan.

That began changing a decade ago in the soccer-ball
60 industry, when Nike, Puma, and Adidas, among others, worked with the International Labor Organization (ILO) and Sialkot suppliers to eradicate child labor. Today a majority of soccer-ball manufacturers voluntarily participate in IMAC's child-labor

monitoring program, but some contest how effective those measures have been.

The case of Saga Sports, in which two children were found working in the home of a subcontractor in May, is not unusual, points out Mr. Dogar of IMAC. Every morning, Dogar's 12 monitors perform unannounced checks on stitching centers 70 randomly selected by computer. Still, children are found from time to time.

"You cannot do 24-hour surveillance. You cannot cover the whole area," he says.

Nonetheless, he and many others question Nike's decision to leave, given how many families may be losing their livelihood.

"They could have found some alternative way with Saga," says Khawaja Zakauddin, who heads the anti-child labor wing of the Sialkot Chamber of Commerce and Industry. "To go 80 away is the worst solution. If Nike moves from here, these people will have no work."

That's certainly a concern of Hussain Naqui, a decade-long employee in Saga's shipping department. "There will be no more jobs without Nike. I'm especially worried about my children, who are studying," he says.

Some say that Nike could have done more. Adidas maintains its own internal monitoring cell in Sialkot; Nike does not, observers say.

"They have to have a transparent monitoring mechanism.[2] 90 It is not just the government or local administration that should be held responsible [for monitoring]. Nike is also responsible," says Kailash Satyarthi, chairman of the Global March Against Child Labor in New Delhi.

Others disagree. "The primary responsibility lies with the government," argues Kaiser Bengali, an economist in Karachi.

---

[2] **transparent monitoring mechanism:** holding corporations responsible for their actions, and making their practices visible to the public

© Houghton Mifflin Harcourt Publishing Company

Mr. Bengali hopes the incident will prove a wakeup call for the country, resulting in better enforcement of child-labor laws, which remain weak even though Pakistan has ratified ILO and United Nations conventions against child labor.

100   Many here in Sialkot worry that Saga's fall could chip away at a decade of progress: Low unemployment, stability, and a private sector that pours money into schools, clinics, and roads.

"There is no link to terrorist activity here, because everyone is involved in their work," says Khurram A. Khawaja, Chief Executive of Anwar Khawaja Industries, which produces soccer balls for Select Sports in Denmark. "This will create a void."

Am I on Track?

Actual Time Spent Reading

This Company Is Employing Children?

Let's boycott their products! Or better not?

by Nadira Faulmüller, Oxford University   *November 15, 2012*

NOTES

Regularly, media reports reveal that Western companies have children working in their factories in Third or Second World countries—may it be for clothing, furniture or, as recently, technical gadgets. Such reports are often followed by people calling for a boycott of the company's products.

"Work done by children" is an extremely broad expression. There is nothing else than to vehemently fight against "work" that goes along with gross abuse like forced labour, carrying heavy weights or any other activity putting a child's physical or
10   mental wellbeing in danger.

But also in cases where no such exploitation is taking place, we have good arguments against children doing work. We fear they might be "the cheapest to hire, the easiest to fire, and the least likely to protest." And we don't want them to be deprived of the opportunity to get a proper education.

So what should we do if we read media reports about a company employing minors? Even if we don't know the exact circumstances, joining a boycott of this company's products can't be wrong, can it?

20   It can. Even if a boycott is well-intentioned, on a practical level it might be wrong to force companies to dismiss their child workers. The main cause for children doing work is poverty— "their survival, and that of their families, depend on it." Earning money is an unavoidable necessity for them. If they must give up their jobs in Western companies, they are forced to exchange them for something else—and this might not be to their advantage. For example, when the U.S. Congress threatened to ban the import of clothing made by children under 14 in Bangladesh, around 50,000 of them went from their jobs in the
30   relatively clean textile factories to collecting garbage. Moreover,

economic modelling research implies that in certain situations product boycotts even can cause child labor to increase rather than decline.

Of course, the consideration that it can become even worse for children is no argument for them working in general. It rather is an argument for a well-considered approach towards this issue. Until we have tackled the problem of general poverty, rather than forcing companies to fire children—may it be via product boycott or regulations—we might think about
40 enforcing safe work conditions for them. Objectively, this might be of greater help for the children involved.

But there is more to that issue than the practical level. On a moral level, many of us still wouldn't want to buy a product manufactured by a child—even if we knew that the work conditions were optimal. We feel that it's simply wrong that the mobile phone we are about to give our teenage daughter was put together by another 14-year-old in India. A dinner party argument *why* this is wrong, I reckon, might come down to something like "Children should not work. This Indian girl is
50 deprived of her childhood if she has to."

I want to suggest by no means that inequality in opportunities and wealth is a good thing to have. However, I feel that there is some sort of arrogance contained in the "children should not work" argument. What childhood is and what it should consist of is *a social construction* to some extent. This construction highly differs between countries and across time. The firm belief that a "proper childhood" does not entail any work is something specific to our time and culture. In other cultures, children are expected to work together with
60 their parents. This happens not only out of financial need, but also as part of the family's work ethics. And even within Western culture, what is seen as a good childhood can vary. Different from other children in the U.S., the Amish are allowed to leave school and start working at around the age of 14.

There is hardly any child unwilling to go to school who doesn't hear the "it's for your own good, it prepares you for

adult life" argument. Couldn't we let count the same argument for work that helps gaining practical skills or is in line with a
70 culture's ethics?

Long story short: If next somebody tries to convince me to boycott a company, I think I shouldn't join in as long as I don't know more about the actual circumstances of the children's work involved—both for practical and moral reasons. What do you think?

Am I on Track?

Actual Time Spent Reading

Part 1 Questions

Answer the following questions. You may refer to your reading notes, and you should cite text evidence in your responses. Your answers to these questions will be scored. You will be able to refer to your answers as you write your essay in Part 2.

1 The word *eradicate* can be found in line 62 of Source #2. Based on the context of the passage, what is a synonym for *eradicate*?

    a. exaggerate

    b. criticize

    c. define

    d. remove

2 **Prose Constructed-Response** What steps did Nike take to end its reliance on child labor? Include support from the sources in your answer.

_____

_____

_____

_____

_____

3 **Prose Constructed-Response** Give two reasons why Nadira Faulmüller in Source #3 hesitates to join boycotts of products made by child labor.

_____

_____

_____

_____

_____

▶ Part 2 (70 minutes)

You will now have 70 minutes to review your notes and sources and to plan, draft, revise, and edit your essay. While you may use your notes and refer to the sources, your essay must represent your original work. You may refer to your responses to the questions in Part 1, but you cannot change those answers. Now read your assignment and the information about how your writing will be scored; then begin your work.

Your Assignment

The debate team is beginning final preparations for its upcoming competition. It is time to start writing your argumentative essay. Remember, your essay should explain whether you agree or disagree with the idea that it is okay to buy products made with child labor. When writing your essay, find ways to use information from the three sources to support your argument. A good argumentative essay should include a strong claim, and it should address opposing arguments.

Argumentative Essay Scoring

Your essay will be scored using the following:

1. **Organization/purpose:** How well did you express your claim, address opposing claims, and support your claim with logical ideas? How well did your ideas flow from beginning to end? How effective was your introduction and conclusion?

2. **Evidence/elaboration:** How well did you incorporate relevant information from the sources? Did you use specific titles or numbers in referring to the sources? How strong is the elaboration for your ideas? Did you clearly state your ideas in your own words in a way that is appropriate for your audience and purpose?

3. **Conventions:** How well did you follow the rules of grammar, punctuation, capitalization, and spelling?

Now begin work on your essay. Manage your time carefully so that you can:

- plan your essay, using your notes

- write your essay

- revise and edit your final draft

RESEARCH SIMULATION

Informative Essay

A medical company in your community is sponsoring an essay contest about the history of medicine. You are entering the contest and have decided to write an informative essay about how penicillin came to be used as medicine.

First you will review three articles about the discovery of the bacteria-fighting properties of penicillin. After you have reviewed these sources, you will answer some questions about them. You should first skim the sources and the questions and then go back and read them carefully.

In Part 2, you will write an informative essay that explains the events that led to penicillin's being used as medicine.

Time Management: Informative Task

There are two parts to most formal writing tests. Both parts of the tests are timed, so it's important to use your limited time wisely.

Part 1: Read Sources and Answer Questions

Preview the Assignment

35 minutes

You will have 35 minutes to read three texts about penicillin. You will also answer questions that will help you plan your essay on the topic.

35 minutes! That's not much time.

How Many?

How many pages of reading?

How many multiple-choice questions?

How many prose constructed-response questions?

Preview the questions. This will help you know which information you'll need to find as you read.

How do you plan to use the 35 minutes?

Estimated time to read:

Source #1: "Not-So-Dumb Luck"		minutes
Source #2: "The History of Penicillin"		minutes
Source #3: "The Discovery of Penicillin"		minutes
Estimated time to answer questions?		minutes
Total	**35**	**minutes**

This is a lot to do in a short time.

Important Hint! As you read the sources, underline, circle, and take notes. You may not have time to reread.

Any concerns?

_____

_____

_____

Part 2: Write the Essay

70

How much time do you have? Pay attention to the clock.

Plan and Write an Informative Essay

→ **70 minutes**

You will have 70 minutes to plan, write, revise, and edit your essay.

Your Plan

Before you start to write, decide on your precise claim and reasons. Then think about the evidence you will use to support your reasons.

How do you plan to use the 70 minutes?

Estimated time for planning the essay?		minutes
Estimated time for writing?		minutes
Estimated time for editing?		minutes
Estimated time for checking spelling, grammar, and punctuation?		minutes
Total	**70**	**minutes**

Be sure to leave enough time for this step.

Notes:

_____

_____

_____

_____

Reread your essay, making sure that the points are clear. Check that there are no spelling or punctuation mistakes.

▶ Your Task

> You are entering an essay contest concerning the
> history of medicine, and you have chosen the topic
> of penicillin. You will write an informative essay about
> the events that led to the discovery and development
> of penicillin. In researching the topic, you have
> identified three sources you will use in planning your
> informative essay.

After you have reviewed the sources, you will answer some questions
about them. Briefly skim the sources and the three questions that
follow. Then, go back and read the sources carefully so you will have the
information you will need to answer the questions. Take notes on the
sources as you read. You may refer back to your notes at any time during
Part 1 or Part 2 of the performance task.

▶ Part 1 (35 minutes)

You will now read the sources. After carefully reading the sources, use
the rest of the time in Part 1 to answer the three questions about them.
Though your answers to these questions will help you think about what
you have read and plan your essay, they will also be scored as part of
the test.

SOURCE #1:
Not-So-Dumb Luck

by Jesse Lane

© Houghton Mifflin Harcourt Publishing Company

NOTES

Potato chips were invented because a hotel guest in Saratoga Springs, NY, demanded a crispier, tastier fried potato.

The goo now known as Silly Putty was a huge success, but it was originally developed as a synthetic rubber during World War II.

Corn Flakes were invented by the Kellogg brothers in their search for a healthy vegetarian snack that hospital patients could eat instead of bread.

Velcro was invented when George de Mestral noticed how
10 certain types of burrs would cling to his clothes and his dog's fur whenever he took him for a walk in the woods.

Necessity is not always the mother of invention; sometimes it's happenstance that begets the most amazing discoveries. Arguably one of the greatest medical discoveries of all time— the invention of penicillin—was discovered completely by accident.

When bacteriologist Alexander Fleming left for vacation one day in September of 1928, he left a mess in his laboratory. When he came back, he noticed that every dish he had left
20 out in the open was covered in mold. He examined each dish closely to see if any hadn't been contaminated. Suddenly, Fleming's attention was drawn to one particular petri dish.

The dish that had caught Fleming's eye contained a *staphylococci* culture—in other words, it was chock full of bacteria—and while Fleming had been away, the culture had also grown a tuft of yellow-green mold. When he peered into the dish, Fleming saw a ring around the mold. After some experimentation, he found that the ring was bacteria-free, and that the mold was a rare spore called *Penicillium notatum*,
30 which had wafted on air currents into his lab from another floor.

Fleming's discovery was born from sheer luck—and yet, he and two other scientists named Howard Florey and Ernst Boris Chain (a pathologist and biochemist, respectively)—went on to win the Nobel Prize in Medicine in 1945. Perhaps the most compelling fact about penicillin is that it went on to save hundreds of thousands of lives during World War II, and has continued to forestall infectious diseases ever since.

Am I on Track?

Actual Time Spent Reading

The History of Penicillin

by Mary Bellis, About.com Guide

Penicillin is one of the earliest discovered and widely used antibiotic agents, derived from the Penicillium mold. Antibiotics are natural substances that are released by bacteria and fungi into the their environment, as a means of inhibiting other organisms—it is chemical warfare on a microscopic scale.

History of Penicillin

Originally noticed by a French medical student, Ernest Duchesne, in 1896. Penicillin was re-discovered by bacteriologist Alexander Fleming working at St. Mary's Hospital in London in 1928. He observed that a plate culture of
10 Staphylococcus had been contaminated by a blue-green mold and that colonies of bacteria adjacent to the mold were being dissolved. Curious, Alexander Fleming grew the mold in a pure culture and found that it produced a substance that killed a number of disease-causing bacteria. Naming the substance penicillin, Dr. Fleming in 1929 published the results of his investigations, noting that his discovery might have therapeutic value if it could be produced in quantity.

Dr. Howard Florey

It was not until 1939 that Dr. Howard Florey, a future Nobel Laureate, and three colleagues at Oxford University began
20 intensive research and were able to demonstrate penicillin's ability to kill infectious bacteria. As the war with Germany continued to drain industrial and government resources, the British scientists could not produce the quantities of penicillin needed for clinical trials on humans and turned to the United States for help. They were quickly referred to the Peoria Lab where scientists were already working on fermentation methods to increase the growth rate of fungal cultures. One July 9, 1941, Howard Florey and Norman Heatley, Oxford University Scientists came to the U.S. with a small but valuable package
30 containing a small amount of penicillin to begin work.

Pumping air into deep vats containing corn steep liquor (a non-alcoholic by-product of the wet milling process) and the addition of other key ingredients was shown to produce faster growth and larger amounts of penicillin than the previous surface-growth method. Ironically, after a worldwide search, it was a strain of penicillin from a moldy cantaloupe in a Peoria market that was found and improved to produce the largest amount of penicillin when grown in the deep vat, submerged conditions.

Andrew J. Moyer

40 By November 26, 1941, Andrew J. Moyer, the lab's expert on the nutrition of molds, had succeeded, with the assistance of Dr. Heatley, in increasing the yields of penicillin 10 times. In 1943, the required clinical trials were performed and penicillin was shown to be the most effective antibacterial agent to date. Penicillin production was quickly scaled up and available in quantity to treat Allied soldiers wounded on D-Day. As production was increased, the price dropped from nearly priceless in 1940, to $20 per dose in July 1943, to $0.55 per dose by 1946.

50 As a result of their work, two members of the British group were awarded the Nobel Prize. Dr. Andrew J. Moyer from the Peoria Lab was inducted into the Inventors Hall of Fame and both the British and Peoria Laboratories were designated as International Historic Chemical Landmarks.

Andrew J. Moyer Patent

On May 25, 1948, Andrew J. Moyer was granted a patent for a method of the mass production of penicillin.

Am I on Track?

Actual Time Spent Reading

SOURCE #3:
The Discovery of Penicillin:
The True Story

by Brittany Connors

Alexander Fleming is credited with the discovery of penicillin, however accidental the discovery actually was. The standard story holds that Fleming had gone on a month-long vacation, and while away, a stray mold spore came through an open window and landed on one of the many bacterial cultures Fleming had not put away before he left. Fleming often admitted that he discovered penicillin by accident, and that all of the work was done by nature. A series of chance events led to the moment of the discovery, however, and not all of them were

10   natural.

It is somewhat suspect that one stray mold spore could have been responsible for the creation of penicillin. Indeed, it is unlikely that a spore would land on a particular culture through a window that, upon further examination, was found not to open. Additionally, penicillin would not have grown under the conditions in Fleming's lab. So, what happened?

Fleming wasn't known for keeping a neat or orderly lab, so it would not have been unusual for open cultures to be scattered about his workspace. Downstairs from Fleming's lab, there was

20   a mycology[1] lab. The mold most likely originated from here, and, based on Fleming's lack of cleanliness, it's possible that one of these mold spores would interact with one of the cultures.

Fleming did not immediately notice the mold's effect when he returned from his vacation in 1928. He had put the cultures in a tray of Lysol to soak after briefly looking them over. When a former lab member came to visit, Fleming showed him some of the cultures. He happened to grab the now-renowned culture from the top of the stack. As he showed it to his former lab assistant, he noticed that the mold on that particular culture

30   looked different than the mold on the other cultures. It seemed that as it had grown, the mold had killed the bacteria in the

NOTES

---

[1] **mycology:** study of mushrooms, molds, and yeasts

culture. His interest aroused, Fleming spent a few weeks both trying to discover what exactly had killed the bacteria and trying to grow more of the mold. In 1929, he wrote a paper on his findings—that penicillin was the antibacterial agent in the mold. However, Fleming wasn't able to determine how to use the penicillin in humans.

In 1938, Howard Florey and Ernst Chain began to study penicillin. They believed there was medical potential in
40 penicillin. Florey and Chain were working on their research in earnest in 1939 and 1940, during World War II. Part of the reason for their increased effort in discovering how penicillin could be used on humans was that a drug was needed to reduce bacterial infections in soldiers' wounds. When they finally determined a way for penicillin to be safely administered to humans, the drug was mass-produced and used on the war front. It saved many lives.

In 1945, Florey, Chain, and Fleming were awarded the Nobel Prize in Physiology or Medicine. Despite Florey and
50 Chain's application of Fleming's work, Fleming alone is credited with penicillin's discovery. He may have called noticing the famous culture a simple accident, but it was a series of many events that led to penicillin being widely used today as an effective medicine.

Am I on Track?

Actual Time Spent Reading

Part 1 Questions

Answer the following questions. You may refer to your reading notes, and you should cite text evidence in your responses. Your answers to these questions will be scored. You will be able to refer to your answers as you write your essay in Part 2.

1 Which of the following is a claim one could make after reading these three sources?

    a. Penicillin prevents bacteria from reproducing.

    b. The discovery of penicillin was not at all accidental.

    c. Alexander Fleming was the first scientist to observe penicillin.

    d. The discovery of penicillin changed modern medicine.

2 **Prose Constructed-Response** What role did luck play in Alexander Fleming's discovery of penicillin? Include support from the sources in your answer.

_____

_____

_____

_____

_____

3 **Prose Constructed-Response** Why did Howard Florey and Ernst Chain do serious research on penicillin in 1939 and 1940?

_____

_____

_____

_____

_____

Part 2 (70 minutes)

You now have 70 minutes to review your notes and sources and to plan, draft, revise, and edit your essay. While you may use your notes and refer to the sources, your essay must represent your original work. You may also refer to your responses to the questions in Part 1, but you cannot change those answers. Now read your assignment and the information about how your writing will be scored; then begin your work.

Your Assignment

The deadline for the essay contest is approaching, and so it is time for you to begin writing your informative essay about the discovery and use of penicillin as medicine. As you write your informative essay, make sure that you are including information from the three sources and that you are presenting your ideas in a logical way.

Informative Essay Scoring

Your essay will be scored using the following:

1. **Organization/purpose:** How well did you state your thesis and support your thesis with a logical progression of ideas? Did you use a variety of transitions between ideas? Was your focus narrow enough to lead to a well-formed conclusion?

2. **Evidence/elaboration:** How well did you incorporate relevant information from the sources? How well did you elaborate your ideas? Did you use precise language appropriate to your audience and purpose?

3. **Conventions:** How well did you follow the rules of grammar, punctuation, capitalization, and spelling?

Now begin work on your essay. Manage your time carefully so that you can:

- plan your essay, using your notes
- write your essay
- revise and edit your final draft

TASK 3

Literary Analysis

Your English and history teachers are working together to teach a unit on the American Revolution. Your class has been assigned a literary analysis of two essays and a poem about the actions of Paul Revere.

First you will review the three sources. After you have reviewed these sources, you will answer some questions about them. You should first skim the sources and the questions and then go back and read them carefully.

In Part 2, you will write a literary analysis in which you compare the real-life events as they are described in the essays to the way they are presented in the poem.

Time Management: Literary Analysis Task

There are two parts to most formal writing tests. Both parts of the tests are timed, so it's important to use your limited time wisely.

Part 1: Read Sources and Answer Questions

Preview the Assignment

35 minutes

You will have 35 minutes to read two essays and a narrative poem about Paul Revere's famous ride. You will also answer questions that will help you plan your literary analysis.

35 minutes! That's not much time.

How Many?

How many pages of reading?

How many multiple-choice questions?

How many prose constructed-response questions?

Preview the questions. This will help you know which information you'll need to find as you read.

How do you plan to use the 35 minutes?

Estimated time to read:

    Source #1: "Paul Revere and the American Revolution" ___ minutes

    Source #2: "Paul Revere's Ride" ___ minutes

    Source #3: "How Accurate Was Longfellow's Poem?" ___ minutes

Estimated time to answer questions? ___ minutes

Total   **35 minutes**

This is a lot to do in a short time.

Important Hint!
As you read the sources, underline, circle, and take notes.
You may not have time to reread.

Any concerns?

_____

_____

Part 2: Write the Analysis

70

How much time do you have? Pay attention to the clock.

Plan and Write a Literary Analysis

70 minutes

You will have 70 minutes to plan, write, revise, and edit your literary analysis.

Your Plan

Before you start writing, decide how you will organize your literary analysis:

Point-by-Point? ☐   Subject-by-Subject? ☐

How do you plan to use the 70 minutes?

Be sure to leave enough time for this step.

Estimated time for planning the essay?		minutes
Estimated time for writing?		minutes
Estimated time for editing?		minutes
Estimated time for checking spelling, grammar, and punctuation?		minutes
Total	**70**	**minutes**

Notes:

_____

_____

_____

_____

Reread your essay, making sure that the points are clear. Check that there are no spelling or punctuation mistakes.

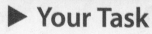

▶ Your Task

> Your class is doing a literary analysis of a historical poem by Henry Wadsworth Longfellow. You are to analyze the poem using two essays that describe the events depicted in the poem. You will work with all three sources to write an analysis that compares and contrasts the way the events are presented in the essays with the way they are presented in the poem.

After you have reviewed the sources, you will answer some questions about them. Briefly skim the sources and the three questions that follow. Then, go back and read the sources carefully so you will have the information you will need to answer the questions. Take notes on the sources as you read. You may refer back to your notes at any time during Part 1 or Part 2 of the performance task.

▶ Part 1 (35 minutes)

You will now read the sources. After carefully reading the sources, use the rest of the time in Part 1 to answer the questions about them. Though your answers to these questions will help you think about what you have read and plan your essay, they will also be scored as part of the test.

© Houghton Mifflin Harcourt Publishing Company

Paul Revere
and the American Revolution

by Ethel Ames

Paul Revere (1735–1818) was a successful silversmith and American patriot from Massachusetts who took an active part in the events leading up to the American Revolution. He assisted the colonies' cause by gathering and reporting information on the movement of British troops.

On the evening of April 18, 1775, Revere was sent to Lexington to warn the American leaders Samuel Adams and John Hancock that British troops were on their way to arrest them and seize weapons being stored in Concord. First Revere
10 was rowed across the Charles River to Charlestown and then he rode through Somerville, Medford, and Arlington, warning citizens along the way of the approaching British troops.

A second rider, William Dawes, rode out to Lexington as well, via a different route. After the message was successfully delivered, Revere, Dawes, and a third rider, Samuel Prescott, went on to nearby Concord. British troops stopped Revere and Dawes, but Prescott got through and was able to warn the Concord Patriots to hide their guns and supplies.

The Battles of Lexington and Concord began early in the
20 morning of April 19 as British troops arrived to face Americans who had already been warned of their approach. These were the first military engagements of the American Revolutionary War. In a poem, Ralph Waldo Emerson described the first shot by an American patriot as the "shot heard 'round the world."

Am I on Track?

Actual Time Spent Reading

Paul Revere's Ride

by Henry Wadsworth Longfellow

NOTES

Listen, my children, and you shall hear
Of the midnight ride of Paul Revere,
On the eighteenth of April, in Seventy-five;
Hardly a man is now alive
5   Who remembers that famous day and year.

He said to his friend, "If the British march
By land or sea from the town to-night,
Hang a lantern aloft in the belfry arch
Of the North Church tower as a signal light,—

10   One if by land, and two, if by sea;
And I on the opposite shore will be,
Ready to ride and spread the alarm
Through every Middlesex village and farm,
For the country folk to be up and to arm."

15   Then he said "Good-night!" and with muffled oar
Silently rowed to the Charlestown shore,
Just as the moon rose over the bay,
Where swinging wide at her moorings lay
The Somerset, British man-of-war;
20   A phantom ship, with each mast and spar
Across the moon like a prison bar,
And a huge black hulk, that was magnified
By its own reflection in the tide.

Meanwhile, his friend through alley and street
25 Wanders and watches, with eager ears,
Till in the silence around him he hears
The muster of men at the barrack door,
The sound of arms, and the tramp of feet,
And the measured tread of the grenadiers,
30 Marching down to their boats on the shore.

Then he climbed the tower of the Old North Church,
By the wooden stairs, with stealthy tread,
To the belfry-chamber overhead,
And startled the pigeons from their perch
35 On the sombre rafters, that round him made
Masses and moving shapes of shade,—
By the trembling ladder, steep and tall,
To the highest window in the wall,
Where he paused to listen and look down
40 A moment on the roofs of the town
And the moonlight flowing over all.

Beneath, in the churchyard, lay the dead,
In their night-encampment on the hill,
Wrapped in silence so deep and still
45 That he could hear, like a sentinel's tread,
The watchful night-wind, as it went
Creeping along from tent to tent,
And seeming to whisper, "All is well!"
A moment only he feels the spell
50 Of the place and the hour, and the secret dread
Of the lonely belfry and the dead;
For suddenly all his thoughts are bent
On a shadowy something far away,
Where the river widens to meet the bay,-
55 A line of black that bends and floats
On the rising tide, like a bridge of boats.

Meanwhile, impatient to mount and ride,
Booted and spurred, with a heavy stride
On the opposite shore walked Paul Revere.
60 Now he patted his horse's side,
Now he gazed at the landscape far and near,
Then, impetuous, stamped the earth,
And turned and tightened his saddle-girth;
But mostly he watched with eager search
65 The belfry-tower of the Old North Church,
As it rose above the graves on the hill,
Lonely and spectral and somber and still.
And lo! as he looks, on the belfry's height
A glimmer, and then a gleam of light!
70 He springs to the saddle, the bridle he turns,
But lingers and gazes, till full on his sight
A second lamp in the belfry burns!

A hurry of hoofs in a village street,
A shape in the moonlight, a bulk in the dark,
75 And beneath, from the pebbles, in passing, a spark
Struck out by a steed flying fearless and fleet:
That was all! And yet, through the gloom and the light,
The fate of a nation was riding that night;
And the spark struck out by that steed, in his flight,
80 Kindled the land into flame with its heat.

He has left the village and mounted the steep,
And beneath him, tranquil and broad and deep,
Is the Mystic, meeting the ocean tides;
And under the alders that skirt its edge,
85 Now soft on the sand, now loud on the ledge,
Is heard the tramp of his steed as he rides.

It was twelve by the village clock
When he crossed the bridge into Medford town.
He heard the crowing of the cock,
90 And the barking of the farmer's dog,
And felt the damp of the river fog,
That rises after the sun goes down.

It was one by the village clock,
When he galloped into Lexington.
95 He saw the gilded weathercock
Swim in the moonlight as he passed,
And the meeting-house windows, blank and bare,
Gaze at him with a spectral glare,
As if they already stood aghast
100 At the bloody work they would look upon.

It was two by the village clock,
When he came to the bridge in Concord town.
He heard the bleating of the flock,
And the twitter of birds among the trees,
105 And felt the breath of the morning breeze
Blowing over the meadow brown.
And one was safe and asleep in his bed
Who at the bridge would be first to fall,
Who that day would be lying dead,
110 Pierced by a British musket-ball.

You know the rest. In the books you have read,
How the British Regulars fired and fled,—
How the farmers gave them ball for ball,
From behind each fence and farm-yard wall,
115   Chasing the red-coats down the lane,
Then crossing the fields to emerge again
Under the trees at the turn of the road,
And only pausing to fire and load.

So through the night rode Paul Revere;
120   And so through the night went his cry of alarm
To every Middlesex village and farm,—
A cry of defiance, and not of fear,
A voice in the darkness, a knock at the door,
And a word that shall echo forevermore!
125   For, borne on the night-wind of the Past,
Through all our history, to the last,
In the hour of darkness and peril and need,
The people will waken and listen to hear
The hurrying hoof-beats of that steed,
130   And the midnight message of Paul Revere.

Am I on Track?

Actual Time Spent Reading

SOURCE #3:
How Accurate Was
Longfellow's Poem?

by Franklin Johnson

Henry Wadsworth Longfellow wrote his poem "Paul Revere's Ride" in 1860, during the turbulent times when the United States was on the brink of civil war. Commentators have pointed out the many of the historical details he got wrong. For example, the lantern signal was not to inform Revere of which route the British were taking, but to let others know in case Revere was captured. Longfellow didn't mention Dawes and Prescott—two other riders on the same mission that night in 1775.

10 Perhaps he got the details wrong because the events were already 85 years in the past. Or, it is equally likely that Longfellow didn't care as much about historical accuracy as he did about creating a vivid picture of a patriot who acted bravely to arouse the country when a terrible danger was at hand.

For Longfellow—an abolitionist—the division of the United States and the impending war over slavery was as dangerous and threatening to America as the British troops were in 1775. Longfellow describes Revere's actions in heroic terms in an effort to rouse patriots from a deep indifference and tell them
20 that they may soon be called upon to act heroically themselves.

Thanks to Longfellow, Paul Revere became once more a national hero and legend. His name is still invoked by politicians and leaders of all stripes. For example, in 1967, during the civil rights struggle, the Rev. Dr. Martin Luther King Jr. said, "We still need some Paul Revere of conscience to alert every hamlet and every village of America that revolution is still at hand."

Am I on Track?

Actual Time Spent Reading

Part 1 Questions

Answer the following questions. You may refer to your reading notes, and you should cite text evidence in your responses. Your answers to these questions will be scored. You will be able to refer to your answers as you write your essay in Part 2.

1 Read this sentence from Source #3:

"Longfellow describes Revere's actions in heroic terms in an effort to rouse patriots from a deep indifference and tell them that they may soon be called upon to act heroically themselves."

Which of the following is a synonym for *indifference* as it is used in the sentence?

   a. disregard
   b. madness
   c. activity
   d. temperament

2 Which of the following details is historically accurate?

   a. Paul Revere was the only American who warned citizens about the British troops.
   b. Paul Revere told Samuel Adams and John Hancock that British troops intended to arrest them.
   c. A lantern signal was used to inform Paul Revere of the route the British were taking.
   d. William Dawes and Samuel Prescott were captured by British troops, but Paul Revere was not.

3 **Prose Constructed-Response** Based on the information in Source #3, explain why Longfellow's poem includes historical inaccuracies. Cite specific evidence from the text to support your answer.

_____

_____

_____

_____

_____

_____

_____

_____

_____

_____

_____

_____

_____

_____

_____

_____

▶ Part 2 (70 minutes)

You now have 70 minutes to review your notes and sources and to plan, draft, revise, and edit your essay. While you may use your notes and refer to the sources, your essay must represent your original work. You may also refer to your responses to the questions in Part 1, but you cannot change those answers. Now read your assignment and the information about how your writing will be scored; then begin your work.

Your Assignment

Your teacher has asked the class to begin writing their literary analyses. Think about how the same historical events are presented in the poem and the essays. As you write your analysis, use information from the essays to comment on the historical accuracy of the poem. Make sure that you include textual evidence from all three sources to support your claims.

Literary Analysis Scoring

Your literary analysis will be scored using the following:

1. **Organization/purpose:** How well did you state your thesis/controlling idea and support it with a logical progression of ideas? Did you use a variety of transitions between ideas? Was your controlling idea narrow enough to lead to a logical conclusion?

2. **Evidence/elaboration:** How well did you incorporate relevant information from the literary texts? How well did you elaborate your ideas? Did you use precise language appropriate to your audience and purpose?

3. **Conventions:** How well did you follow the rules of grammar, punctuation, capitalization, and spelling?

Now begin work on your essay. Manage your time carefully so that you can:

- plan your essay, using your notes
- write your essay
- revise and edit your final draft

Acknowledgments

"The History of Penicillin" by Mary Bellis from *About.com*, http:inventors.about.com. Text copyright © 2013 by Mary Bellis. Reprinted by permission of About, Inc.

"How a Sonnet Turned a Statue Into the 'Mother of Exiles'" by Sam Roberts from *The New York Times,* October 27, 2011. Text copyright © 2011 by The New York Times. Reprinted by permission of PARS International on behalf of The New York Times.

"How Many Active Volcanoes Are There in the World?" (Retitled: "How Many Active Volcanoes Are There?") by T. Simkin and L. Siebert from *Smithsonian,* http://www.volcano.si.edu. Text copyright © 2002-2013 by Smithsonian. Reprinted by permission of Smithsonian.

Excerpt from "Ka`u Scenic Byway—the Slopes of Mauna Loa" (Retitled: "On the Slopes of Mauna Loa, Hawaii Island") by Marge Elwell, from the *Hawaii Department of Transportation,* www.hawaiiscenicbyways.org. Text copyright © 2013 by Ka'u Scenic Byway Committee. Reprinted by permission of the Ka'u Scenic Byway Committee.

"Kidnap Poem" from *The Selected Poems of Nikki Giovanni* by Nikki Giovanni. Text copyright © 1996 by Nikki Giovanni. Reprinted by permission of HarperCollins Publishers.

"Nike Pledges to End Child Labor and Apply U.S. Rules Abroad" by John H. Cushman from *The New York Times,* May 13, 1998. Text copyright © 1998 by The New York Times. Reprinted by permission of PARS International on behalf of The New York Times.

"Nike's Dilemma: Is Doing the Right Thing Wrong?" by David Montero from *The Christian Science Monitor,* December 22, 2006. Text copyright © 2006 by The Christian Science Monitor. Reprinted by permission of The Christian Science Monitor.

"Sacrificing the First Amendment to Catch Cyberbullies" by Linda Wertheimer & Linda Sanchez from *The Cornell Law School Federalist Society,* October 10, 2011, www.cornellfedsoc.org. Text copyright © 2011 by Cornell Law School Federalist Society. Reprinted by permission of Cornell Law School Federalist Society.

"This Company is Employing Children? Let's Boycott Their Products! Or Better Not?" by Nadira Faulmüller from the *Oxford Centre for Practical Ethics,* November 15, 2012, www.blog.practicalethics.ox.uk. Text copyright © 2012 by Nadira Faulmüller. Reprinted by permission of Nadira Faulmüller.

"What is Cyberbullying?" by Leigh Anne Kraemer-Naser from *The Ophelia Project,* www.opheliaproject.org. Text copyright © 2011 by The Ophelia Project. Reprinted by permission of The Ophelia Project.

"Why Waste Time on a Foreign Language?" by Jay Mathews from *The Washington Post,* April 22, 2010. Text copyright © 2010 by The Washington Post. Reprinted by permission of PARS International on behalf of The Washington Post.